Mind, Brain, and Consciousness

The Neuropsychology of Cognition

PERSPECTIVES IN
NEUROLINGUISTICS AND PSYCHOLINGUISTICS

Harry A. Whitaker, Series Editor
DEPARTMENT OF PSYCHOLOGY
THE UNIVERSITY OF ROCHESTER
ROCHESTER, NEW YORK

HAIGANOOSH WHITAKER and HARRY A. WHITAKER (Eds.).
  Studies in Neurolinguistics, Volumes 1 and 2; Volume 3. In preparation
NORMAN J. LASS (Ed.). Contemporary Issues in Experimental Phonetics
JASON W. BROWN. Mind, Brain, and Consciousness: The Neuropsychology
  of Cognition

In preparation

I. M. SCHLESINGER and LILA NAMIR (Eds.). Sign Language of the Deaf:
  Psychological, Linguistic, and Sociological Perspectives
S. J. SEGALOWITZ and F. A. GRUBER (Eds.). Language Development and
  Neurological Theory
JOHN MACNAMARA (Ed.). Language Learning and Thought

Mind, Brain, and Consciousness

The Neuropsychology of Cognition

JASON BROWN

Department of Neurology
New York University Medical Center

(AP) ACADEMIC PRESS   New York San Francisco London   1977

A Subsidiary of Harcourt Brace Jovanovich, Publishers

ACADEMIC PRESS, INC.
111 Fifth Avenue, New York, New York 10003

United Kingdom Edition published by
ACADEMIC PRESS, INC. (LONDON) LTD.
24/28 Oval Road, London NW1

Library of Congress Cataloging in Publication Data

Brown, Jason W
     Mind, brain, and consciousness.

     (Perspectives in neurolinguistics and psycholin-
guistics)
          Bibliography: p.
          Includes index.
          1.   Neuropsychiatry—Philosophy.   2.   Higher ner-
vous activity.   3.   Cognition.   4.   Consciousness.
I.   Title.   [DNLM: 1.   Cognition.   2.   Neurophysiology.   WL102   B882m]
RC343.B75   616.8'9'071   76-30311
ISBN 0−12−137550−1

To Jo-Ann

Contents

Preface

It is my belief that there is an underlying order, a lawfulness, to the diversity of symptoms that we observe in patients with functional or organic brain disorder, and that this order reflects the organization of systems that support or in some way generate normal function. In other words, the pattern of dissolution of the normal system determines the symptoms of pathological behavior. According to this thinking, the pathological becomes a clue—actually a key—to an understanding of normal function.

Working in this way from the pathological to the normal, a structural model of *cognition* is described, meaning by this term not just ideation but the whole matrix of perceptual, motoric, affective, and linguistic contents that enter into every mental act.

The bulk of the evidence in support of this model derives from work in human neuropsychology. The orientation brought to bear on this evidence is that of symptom formation as a phenomenon of destructuration. This concept was initially developed in relation to disorders of language (see Brown, 1972) and is here extended, and further elaborated, to a general model of cognition. Apart, however, from its theoretical claim, it is hoped that this monograph will also provoke some re-thinking of a whole range of neurological and psychiatric disorders and, hopefully, stimulate new investigations of pathological change from the point of view of a destructuration hypothesis.

Unlike neuropsychology, there is a long tradition of structural theorizing in the interpretation of psychiatric symptomatology. However, this tradition, apart from psychoanalytic concepts, has not given rise to a formal description, much less a general sketch, of a theory of (pathological) cognition. Psychoanalysis, though having little to say about the psychoses, which are after all the material for such a theory, is nevertheless a contribution in this direction. Therefore, I have indicated some points of contact between the proposed model and that of the psychoanalytic approach. In this regard, I have been fortunate to be able to discuss various aspects of this monograph with Dr. Silvano Arieti and to participate in seminars with Dr. Andrew Peto of the New York Psychoanalytic Society.

For the writing of this work, my needs have been few, though that is not to say simple, only the freedom from too many other responsibilities and some tenacious colleagues willing to argue with me from time to time. As to the former, I have been fortunate in having the generous support of the Foundations' Fund for Research in Psychiatry during the writing of the major portion of this monograph. As to the latter, I am especially grateful to Dr. Joseph Jaffe of Columbia University in New York and Professor Henri Hecaen of the Centre Neurolinguistique et Neuropsychologique in Paris for their warm hospitality and for many hours of stimulating discussion. I wish also to thank my dear friend, Dr. Stanley Malinovich of Brooklyn College, for clarifying many of the pertinent philosophical issues.

Acknowledgment is made for permission to reprint figures from the following sources:

Figure 1, p. 13: Courtesy of Dr. Paul D. MacLean.

Figure 5, p. 57: From Brown, Jason W., Lateralization and language representation, *Neurology*, 1976 (Feb.), p. 188. Reprinted from Neurology © 1976 by The New York Times Media Company, Inc.

Figure 7, p. 167: Courtesy of Dr. Kosta Zaimov. From Zaimov, Kosta, Aphasie chez un peintre, *l'Encéphale*, 1969, *58* (5), 377–417.

Figure 8, p. 169: From Brown, Jason W., *Aphasia, apraxia, and agnosia*, © 1972 Charles C. Thomas, Figure 2, p. 48.

1

Introduction

*If any man cannot grasp the matter let
him be still and the matter will grasp him.*

Suso

This monograph has its historical roots in a wide-ranging and hetero-
geneous school of early neuropsychiatry that was distinguished chiefly by
an emphasis on the genetic aspects of cognitive pathology. Hughlings
Jackson appears to have been the spiritual founder of this school, at least
insofar as one can judge from the continuum existing between his writings
and, for example, those of von Monakow (1914), Pick (1913), Schilder
(1951), and MacLean (1972) in neuropsychology, or the early Freud,
Guiraud (1950), Ey (1950), or Arieti (1967) in psychiatry. The various
works of these authors, though differing in many important respects, share
a common bond in their concept of evolutionary levels in cognition.

The model to be proposed in this monograph takes its point of
departure from this central, one might say thematic, element of the

1

Jacksonian view, that of structural levels, and attempts to build from there an outline of the neurological and psychiatric bases of cognition. Specifically, an attempt is made to align the major disorders of neuropsychology with a comparable series of psychopathological states and to interpret both categories of impairment from the standpoint of a unitary structural model of brain function.

A model of this scope is really a psychology of cognition. As such, it should be strong enough to assimilate any psychopathological symptom. These will hold the psychology together and keep it on firm ground. Symptoms should, in fact, be the mortar of the psychology, not just chosen to illustrate this or that theoretical formulation, since the diversity of clinical symptoms is such as to support by the manner of selection almost any a priori assumption. Moreover, problems of physiology, the nature and site of the pathological lesion, the "organic" features of a psychopathological disorder, are not token elements extrinsic to a systemic psychology. The structural organization of cognition is no less dynamic than the psychological systems it supports. Structure needs to be contemplated at each step of the way in the construction of psychological theory. On the other hand, the brain scientist should not be under the delusion that an elucidation of the organic or etiological basis of a symptom is an explanation of the symptom itself. Anatomy may, as Freud said, be destiny, but anatomical interpretations of symptomatology make for poor psychology.

For the most part, the experimental psychologist looks at those effects that are produced by an alteration of the environment of the organism. A stimulus is changed in some way, such as through brief exposure, or the functional capacity of a system is challenged by a difficult task. From the resultant performance, inferences can be made about the normal process. The psychopathologist can also employ such techniques in the study of patients. He has the advantage, however, of being able to observe changes in performance apart from those that occur in the course of testing. The test situation, however carefully designed, always introduces an artificial element.

These reservations apply equally to developmental psychologies. These tend to proceed independently of structural considerations and, to that extent, fail to contribute greatly to our understanding of structure—function relationships. When one considers the matter, it is surprising that *neuro*psychology has not figured more strongly in psychological theory building. How can one explore the nature of perception and the organization of the object world or the thought—language problem without the least interest in the structural and pathological aspects of these processes? It may not be too farfetched to say that the pathological, *sensu latiori*, is our only trustworthy guide to the nature of normal cognitive organization.

Naturally the fruits of a study of pathological change will depend heavily upon the terms of inquiry. For example, the study of populations of subjects, rather than single individuals, is usually considered to be a conventional prerequisite for good investigation. Population studies, however, may actually force us to abandon all hope for a deeper analysis of a problem. The individual character of a symptom, its qualitative aspects and fluctuation under a variety of conditions, those observations that help us to see the inner nature of a phenomenon, can be filtered out by a methodology that only looks at one performance. Population studies are of value chiefly with respect to questions of incidence or frequency that require large-scale sampling, but they are of little aid in the understanding of the symptom itself.

We need more, however, than a closer look at symptom complexes and their pathological correlations. New findings cannot simply be added on to a descriptive inventory. The constant effort toward discovery carries a demand for new concepts, but the setting-up of new concepts involves a reconsideration of some old ones. Of the many traditional views to be questioned in this work, perhaps the most fundamental deals with the nature of organic and functional disease. We often hear of a similarity between *organic* and *functional* states, of the difficulty in distinguishing the two forms of disorder and their broad overlapping. Yet the acknowledgement of this similarity lacks the commitment of a deeper understanding. In all too many instances, it is little more than a disclaimer for closer study.

In the past, the organic—functional was approached from a common viewpoint. As neurology and psychiatry went their separate ways, the inward turn of both fields drew the organic and the functional further apart. Over the years, neurology has moved in the direction of an increasing reductionism. The greater reliance on technological aids has left in its wake a diminishing interest in the qualitative aspects of brain disorder. On the other hand, psychiatry has gone through a long period of didacticism generating many inessential questions with little regard for neurological concepts. Few who have considered the problem would deny that this situation exists. Areas of contact, such as dream research, psychosurgery, limbic function, or depth stimulation, are only the most superficial meeting grounds. The organic—functional still is not approached from a unitary standpoint.

THE NATURE OF THE SYMPTOM

The present work deals chiefly with the pathological, and here our main focus is on the symptom. The symptom is a scientific datum no less than a sine wave or a synaptic cleft. Moreover, it is an event as predictable as any physical happening, given an understanding of the laws of symptom formation. A symptom always occurs in the context of a process of change. This change must be explored as a key to the systems that are damaged and to the normal substrate that lies behind the symptom. There is a need for a kind of depth analysis of the symptom. It should be followed like a friend through many ups and downs, judged by its acquaintances, viewed under many different conditions, and interpreted only after a long observation. Moreover, symptoms never occur in isolation. We may say that, while a *syndrome* is a complex of symptoms, a *symptom* is always part of a syndrome the other elements of which are waiting to be discovered.

What is the meaning of a symptom? Paralysis is a common neurological symptom, but what does paralysis signify? Weakness of an arm, an intention, or a movement? Loss of volitional, spontaneous, or reflex movement? In what sense are movements lost? Is the normal function damaged, suppressed, or blocked? Does it fragment or does it systematically degrade? Are movements composites of finer movements, patterns of movement, or individual muscles? To what extent is insufficiency a reflection of damage to a specific area or of remaining normal brain deprived of that area? We see immediately how inadequate is our understanding of the *pathological.* Can we proceed from here to an inference about the physiology of *normal* movement?

The problem with an interpretation of paralysis along conventional lines has to do with the inferred chain-like nature of the processes involved. Given a series of stages in movement production, A → B → C, a lesion at B can either remove function B from the repertoire of performance, block function A, or disinhibit function C; a lesion at B may also bring a disturbed function B to the fore, may allow function A to "overflow," or may fail to activate function C. This concerns only the "extirpation" effect of the lesion, and a similar inventory of possibilities holds in the case of stimulation at B. Does the final symptom reflect function A, B, or C, the disordered action of the entire system ABC, or the rest of the brain *sans* ABC?

What then is a symptom? Does it always reflect a pathology or are there "symptoms" of normal function? In states of pathology, a symptom is taken to reflect a lesion. Limb weakness is a symptom that reflects a lesion, say, in motor cortex. Presumably, normal strength is a kind of symptom that also refers to some neural substrate. Few would disagree with the statement that normal strength cannot yet be anatomically explained. Why does this not also apply to instances of hemiplegia? This problem of the relationship between the normal and abnormal is compounded when we come to disorders of psychopathology.

In disorders of psychological function, the symptom is a clue to the organization of the patient's world. It is a link between the private space of the patient and that of the examiner; it is a nidus around which a new level of reality has formed. Conversely, reality has a (perhaps) finite number of levels to which symptoms refer. We may say that a symptom is that part of the disorganization that breaks through into the examination.

We may understand the fact that a symptom refers to a new level of organization by returning to the example of hemiparesis with a cortical lesion: Weakness of the limbs is never the sole problem. Defects in serial performance, impaired exploratory activity, apraxic features, and grasping may be present. Sensory impairments may help to determine phenomena of limb neglect, distortion, or hallucination. Disorders of mood, initiative, affect, and insight may occur as well. These are not all proximity effects of the lesion. There is not a progressive incorporation of otherwise discrete functions by an ever-expanding pathology. Rather, the *cognitive structure* of the organism has systematically degraded to a level at which certain of the above phenomena are coextensive. This process of change is called regression and refers to the appearance of stages that are normally only preliminary. These stages have a molar or global character and may also be conceived of as levels of the personality. A symptom or symptom complex has the nature of an emergent. It is the achieved performance level of the individual.

Accordingly, we speak of the *pathological* when there is an unraveling of the normal, and we speak of the *normal* when the pathological achieves a kind of adequacy.

THE CONCEPT OF REGRESSION

It is insufficient to define a symptom as a level in a regressive process without considering in somewhat more detail the nature of psychological regression. The older use of this term had the meaning of a return to an earlier ontogenetic stage. There is also a suggestion of the Jacksonian concept of a pathological dissolution that retraces the backward course of phylogeny. Pathological symptoms, however, do not precisely correspond to stages in the maturational or evolutionary history of the organism. The "return" to an earlier level does not concern the specific content of the symptom, but rather its general form. Ey (1950) has written:

> In conditions where inferior social structures exist (primitive) the psyche remains fixed at *inferior levels of structuring which correspond to this degree of evolution* . . . (and) if the psyche, during its development, passes the stages necessary for its organization, these stages will remain permanently as a structural hierarchy of layers or levels (Schichten). All this takes place as if the evolution through time remains as an infra-structure of the psychic organism.

Regression implies not only a falling back, but also an *outward pressure.* The level reached has an active character; it is an achievement of the organism. This is true even if the "level" appears in a pathological symptom. The levels that are recaptured in pathological change are also stages through which cognitive formation must pass. Cognition involves an incessant recapitulation of these evolutionary (phylogenetic) and developmental (ontogenetic) stages. Accordingly, this process is referred to as *microgenesis.*

The phyletic or Jacksonian concept of levels leads only to the most rudimentary structural formations. The ontogenetic concept helps us to recognize each psychological level as an amalgam of motoric, perceptual, affective, and linguistic components that are intimitely interrelated. The microgenetic approach attempts to bring the structural and the psychological together in the conception of structural layers and cognitive stages more or less instantaneously traversed.

A basic assumption regarding the process of regression is that it is identical in organic and functional disorders. Those cognitive structures that are built up in the brain will decay according to fixed laws. There are characteristic lines of regression (or emergence) in symptom formation. One may explain apparent differences between the organic and the functional by the structural level likely to be involved, the necessity for unilateral or specific bilateral lesion, the rate and magnitude of pathological change, and the pre-existing performance level. There also tends to be a greater fluctuation in the functional disorders from level to level, so that moments of relative clarity may alternate with otherwise regressed forms. This gives one the false impression that there is no true deficit.

The central problem that limits our understanding of the inner identity of functional and organic disorders concerns the presence, in the latter, of a definite brain pathology. Our interpretation of such pathology, however, will be guided by what has been said of the effects of an organic lesion, namely, to induce a regressive change. The view of functional disorders as regression phenomena is well-established despite the elusiveness of any pathological alteration. On the other hand, in the organic disorders, closer attention to this regression effect, as a general consequence of brain pathology, is required.

For the most part, neuropsychological disorders tend to be associated with unilateral pathology. Such a condition is unlikely to be duplicated by a functional disorder in which the "physiological" change points to a more or less symmetrical process. On the other hand, certain types of bilateral involvement can give rise to symptoms of a psychopathological nature. Instances of such cases in the organic series, however, are quite rare and, because of their bilaterality, are often not thoroughly studied. As a general rule, functional disorders point to bilateral change at earlier structural levels; organic disorders point to unilateral change at later structural levels.

Symptoms that occur with lesions of the brain differ according to the location of the lesion and not, ceteris paribus, its etiology. Etiology is important with respect to rate of onset, age and extent of involvement, whether irritative or destructive, unilateral or bilateral, degree of antici-pated recovery, and so on, but if such variables are taken into considera-tion, the essential element proves to be the brain area involved.

The symptom does not result from destruction of an area, a center. Rather, it reflects the disruption of a plane in cognition that is supported in some way by the damaged area. A symptom is the form taken by that disruption. The brain area in question is not the site of a physiological mechanism, but is a medium by means of which cognition may be advanced one stage further. Accordingly, localization takes on the meaning of a correspondence, not between psychological function and brain mecha-nism, but between a stage in cognitive formation (symptom) and the structural level (area) by means of which that stage is realized.

THE SYMPTOM IN PSYCHOANALYSIS

There is another view of the symptom in psychopathology to be discussed. In psychoanalytic theory, a symptom points to a conflict; it is the compromise of this conflict. Freud (1966, **16**: 366) said, "A symptom, like a dream, represents something as fulfilled." The symptom is also a sign of regression, "a satisfaction in the infantile manner." The symptom, therefore, is the product of both dynamic interaction and a return to an earlier level of gratification.

According to psychoanalytic thinking, the lesion in, say, an hysterical paralysis of an arm is an alteration of the conception, the idea, of the arm, and the abolition of the associative accessibility of the conception of the arm (to the conscious ego). The symptom is a manifestation of a new unconscious idea that is produced by an association between two concurrent mental events. This alteration of the idea is also related to an affective displacement. It is of interest that Breuer commented that the physical process behind this idea was the same in content and form whether the idea rose above the threshold of consciousness or remained beneath it.

This concept will receive closer examination in the chapters to follow. One can say, however, that a symptom of a functional disorder is no more explained by the acquisition of a *psychical* association than an organic symptom is explained by the loss or interruption of an *anatomical* association. The very concept of association implies an understanding of the way in which mental contents come into relationship. At present, knowledge of such relationships (not to mention the nature of the "contents" themselves) is at the earliest stage.

In every functional disorder, there are important links to the organic. In a functional paralysis, the symbolic element does not have to be taken only as an indication of intrapsychic conflict. The altered concept (e.g., of the arm) points also to a semantic displacement in cognition. There is a link to certain complex organic states, such as ideational apraxia and the so-called "body-image" disorders, where symbolic features are also present in the symptomatology. Symptom formation in hysteria is also closely related to features of trance-state cognition and retrograde amnesia. The difference between an organic and a functional paralysis is determined not only by the presence or absence of an organic lesion, but also by their different regression *levels* in the developing action component of cognition.

2

Structural Model

The series of levels through which cognition is elaborated recapitulates, to some extent, a sequence of evolutionary plateaus. Moreover, there is a correspondence between each level in the cognitive series and each plateau or stage in the evolutionary sequence, such that it is possible to describe a dynamic formative structure, built up in the course of evolution and continued into maturation, which supports and elaborates the mental life.

This chapter is an introduction to this general concept by means of a sketch of four more or less arbitrary structural levels that will be repeatedly and more systematically encountered in the pages to follow. Each of these levels has an anatomical and a psychic aspect, the former embracing the distribution and physiology of the system, the latter, action, perception, and inner experience. These levels are conceived of, in a sense, as "closed systems" in that each represents, or represented at some point in evolutionary time, an endstage of cognitive development. Each level, however, is also a transitional phase. The incessant flow of cognition, the continual appearance and disappearance of new form at each moment of our waking and sleeping life, are manifestations of the activity of the structure as a whole as it achieves one or another level of realization.

THE IDEA OF ENCEPHALIZATION

The building up of evolutionary structure in the brain, its forward growth, is termed encephalization. Classically, this refers to a process of cephalad expansion and rostral migration of function. For example, Sherrington (1951) has written that encephalization implies a "shifting of function in the brain from older and more primitive to new and more complex parts." In my view, this is a mistaken notion of the encephalization process.

An example of encephalization that is commonly used in support of the displacement idea is the presumed shift of the visual capacity of optic thalamus in man to visual cortex. Evidence for this consists of the different functional deficits that occur in man and cat with natural or experimental lesions at each of these levels, that is, a cat with bilateral occipital lobe removal has a loss of object vision but retains light discrimination, whereas a comparable lesion in man is said to produce total blindness. Marquis (1934) has written:

> In the phylogenetic series there has been a constant and progressive shifting of the visual function from lower to higher centers of the nervous system. With the appearance in mammals of a cerebral cortex, the mesencephalic centers undergo a differentiation which leaves them incapable of mediating all their former visual functions. The cortex assumes a larger and larger share of the control of visual responses in the ascending series of mammals until in man, the pupillary reflex alone remains possible after its destruction.

Patients with bilateral destruction of the visual cortex and cortical "blindness," however, have a complex change in visual perception; vision is qualitatively altered and not simply abolished. Such patients commonly have hallucinatory experiences, which are of central importance in understanding the nature of the perceptual deficit. Although such patients may deny that they are blind, this is usually discounted by the examiner who is unable to demonstrate visual function. Recent studies in animals have shown considerable subcortical vision (e.g., Schneider, 1969), and a human case has been reported (Damasio *et al.*, 1975) of retained perception in a visual field opposite the side of hemispherectomy. These findings indicate the need for a new approach to the problem of perceptual organization (see Chapter 5) and, at the same time, challenge a view of encephalization based on a theory of functional transfer.

A more comprehensive view of this problem was taken by Coghill (1929). He demonstrated, with respect to neuromuscular function, that the phase of cortical elaboration occured *prior* to the capacity to incorporate that elaboration into pre-existing structure. For this reason, one should view encephalization not as an adding on or transfer of function cephalad but as a progressive capacity of cortex to share in pre-existing systems. Encephalization is an expression of evolutionary growth, a process through which each new capacity involves a total change in the neuraxis. Moreover, such capacities do not evolve in a piecemeal fashion but are accompanied by a progressive change in other aspects of cognition as well. A new function is a new cognitive level. Cognition achieves these new forms together with, indeed dependent upon, evolutionary differentiation.

In the old view, for example, Jackson (1932) and Herrick (1948), stages in brain evolution were described in terms of increasing sensori–motor complexity or degrees of freedom from reflex activity. To some extent, this approach still survives even in recent publications (e.g., Riss, 1968, 1972). An alternative approach has been employed by MacLean (1972). Three major structural formations are distinguished, each representing a level or stage in brain-behavior development: a "reptilian," a "limbic" or "paleomammalian," and a "neomammalian" (see Figure 1). These stages are not superimposed on one another like a stack of coins, but rather each new layer is derived from the previous one. Moreover, the derivational pattern is linear and stereodynamic, not simply additive in the Jacksonian sense. There are similarities to Yakovlev's (1948) model, in which the hierarchical organization is conceived not so much in terms of relation-

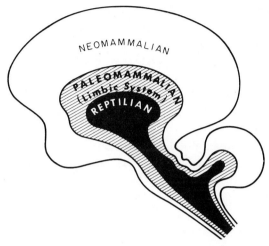

FIGURE 1. Levels in brain evolution and behavior (MacLean, 1972).

ships of subordination, but through a development interaction between three primary spheres of motility.

A STRUCTURAL MODEL OF COGNITION

Of the four levels of structural organization that can be distinguished in man, three are phylogenetic and correspond roughly to stages described by MacLean (1972). The earliest of these is designated the (*1*) *subcortical sensori–motor*, the next the (*2*) *limbic presentational*, the third the (*3*) *cortical representational*. The fourth level, the (*4*) *asymmetric symbolic*, is achieved for the most part in the course of ontogenetic development.

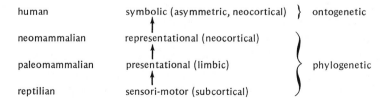

These levels are in no sense "separate brains," but rather they are widely distributed systems that develop *seriatim* out of one another, serving to transform cognition to successively more differentiated states. Moreover, the levels are to some extent arbitrary; each probably comprises several—perhaps innumerable—subsystems. There are not clear transitions from one level to another, since it is not known whether the levels themselves develop as quantal achievements or on a continuum of evolutionary change.

This structure most likely develops out of a foundation of visceral activity, corresponding in part with the innermost visceral stratum in the hierarchy of Yakovlev (1948). The visceral is at the frontier of the transition from the physical to the psychological.

The Sensori–Motor Level

ANATOMICAL ASPECTS

The reptilian forebrain is characterized by a rudimentary cortex. In mammals, this level incorporates much of the reticular formation, midbrain, tectum and basal ganglia, including systems in upper brainstem related to sleep and wakefulness.

In addition, the level embraces other constituents of the extrapyramidal action system, nonspecific thalamic groups and, possibly in primate, centremedian, pulvinar inferior, or, in other mammals, lateralis posterior. The so-called "limbic-midbrain" area in upper brainstem (Nauta, 1958), which is closely related to basal ganglia through prominent pallidotegmental and other connections, is also, in mammals, a part of this level.

BEHAVIOR

In animals, there is evidence that the striatal complex mediates certain "genetically constituted forms of behavior . . . [and] plays a basic part in such behavior as selecting homesite, establishing and defending territory, hunting, homing, mating, rearing young etc. . . ." Lesions of striatum in monkey abolish certain patterns of display (MacLean, 1972). In rostral midbrain, there is a synergic mechanism concerned with emotive display (Brown, 1967). This has been demonstrated in animals for low-threshold facivocal rage by transection, stimulation, and ablation studies and in man for certain aspects of mimetic expression through pathological localizations. Stimulation in free-moving animals has given rise to the concept of a "self-reliant acting system" in the midbrain concerned with affective reactions (Hunsperger, 1956).

The occurrence of *sham rage* as a "stimulation" or "release" phenomenon at this level does not signal a behavioral display lacking in affective content. The precipitant, generalized and labile character of the display, and the lowered threshold and lack of direction are not signs of a behavior in isolation but are manifestations of cognition at this structural level. The organism lives within an immediate somatic space field; the object or target of the action, the stimulus of that action have not yet been differentiated out of a global pre-object.

COGNITION

This represents an initial stage in the emergence of cognition, characteristics of which can be recovered from the study of human psychopathology. The cognitive form is realized in somatic activity centered on the body itself. Sensation is incorporated into a perceptual space model and develops into a generalized, undifferentiated preobject. The space of the perception moves outward from the space of the body, but there is still only a single space field. Motility is effected in axial body-on-body motor patterns as the action accompanies the preobject out into the primitive peri-somatic space field. In fact, we may say that perception, action, and space together reach out into the space around the body. One may conceive of the body as the global somatic referent of the thought that seeks to realize itself in action.

Affect has a drive character. Hunger, sleep, and sexual drive, as instincts rather than their later derivations, can be identified with this stage. Instinct occurs as an advance over reflex. The latter is an occurrence in physical space *outside* of cognition. A reflex is an object for cognition; it comes to cognition as an object and has to be re-created through perceptual development. On the other hand, instinct is early cognition.

Consciousness has proceeded beyond a kind of vegetal activity associated with a purely visceral or autonomic level, but not to the point at which consciousness is articulated by content. Performance is not directed, but rather it is determined by innate factors. There is no "distance" between the perception and the action; both have an immediate, labile, or automatic quality.

As cognition strives toward a further level, each component is transformed. There is an evolution of the pre-object into a more or less well-defined but not yet fully exteriorized image. The space of the developing perception continues to expand. Instincts or drives differentiate into partial expressions centered about these new action and perception forms.

The Limbic-Presentational Level

ANATOMICAL ASPECTS

The paleomammalian stage comprises structures usually included as part of the limbic lobe, namely, hypothalamus, anterior thalamic nuclei, cingulate gyrus, hippocampus, and their interconnections (i.e., the Papez circuit), as well as orbito-frontal, pyriform and perhaps insular cortex, and various subcortical groups, such as amygdala, septal nuclei, and (medial) dorsomedial nucleus of thalamus.

The transitional nature of the various laminar systems which make up the limbic system is well known. These systems appear to represent several phylogenetic planes which, conceivably, may refer to microtemporal levels in cognitive development. Recently, Pandya and Sanides (1973) have demonstrated a progressive emergence, through central zones of differentiation ("growth rings"), of transitional neocortex out of paralimbic motor and parainsular sensory (supplementary) cortex. These may be considered as "cortical representatives" of paleomammalian structures.

BEHAVIOR

For a long time, the limbic lobe was considered to have chiefly an olfactory function. Papez (1937) drew attention to a role in emotional behavior, and subsequently a relation to learning and memory function was demonstrated. The limbic system may also be involved in hallucination. In animals, lesions of limbic structures produce impairments on various cognitive tests (Douglas, 1967). Electroencephalographic studies of the hippocampus in animals suggest participation in states of arousal and learning (Adey, 1961). A range of appetitive states, sexual and other motivated behaviors, changes in aggressiveness or passivity, and fear or anxiety have all been induced through experimental manipulation of limbic structures. Although these various components of behavior may be preferentially altered with lesion or stimulation in different parts of the wider limbic level, the level as a whole is a stage in cognition, not a collection of separate elements.

COGNITION

This level is characterized by a semantic operation through which all emerging contents must pass. There is a transition to a specific content, whether perceptual, motoric, or linguistic. This transition can be thought of as a selectional operation, if by this we mean a striving toward a final form and not a choice between elements. At this level, the object in perception will have the nature of an image since the process leading to the image, or the hallucination, is the same process as that leading to the perception. In fact, the "veridical" perception is an exteriorized image development. The differentiation of the object also corresponds to a differentiation of the forming action pattern which, like the object, proceeds from body-on-body organization in axial and proximal musculature out into the space of the distal limbs. This space field achieves an extrapersonal, but still subjectively intrapsychic, character.

In this manner, cognition proceeds from automatic or reflex-like, and then instinctive, behavior to a type of interpolated delay between a stimulus and a response. This is not a real delay since both the stimulus (perception) and response (action) are carried together outward to a new position in abstract space, drawing the cognitive product still further away from immediate behavior.

The drive character of instinct begins to settle around partial expressions. Anger represents the action-related, fear the perception-related, manifestation of what, at the preceding stage, constituted the hunger—sleep complex. The sexual drive also achieves a similar polarity with aggressive—defensive features. These affects accompany the action and perception as they move out into the object. The action and object have a strong "subjective" flavor. This points to the fact that the content has not fully exteriorized itself to a position in extrapersonal space. To say that the organism incorporates the object, or that an affective or cathectic bond exists with the object, is to say that the object, and all other components which accompany it, have not achieved a status independent of the mind in which they originated.

Awareness achieves a level common to that of dream. The awareness experience takes on direction by virtue of a progression toward an object or an action, but the awareness is still embedded in the object itself. The object does not exist as an entity fully independent of the self. There is incomplete distinction of self and object because they inhabit one space. Possibly some apprehension of time passing can occur at this stage. The isolation of content in an immediate present out of a more or less coterminous background seems to be essential for at least some intuition of duration.

The Cortical-Representational Level

ANATOMY

The neocortical or neomammalian stage comes as a relatively late development with continued expansion over the mammalian series to man. Recent studies have helped to clarify the organization of neocortex from two points of view that are relevant to the present theoretical orientation. The first of these concerns cyto- and myeloarchitectonic studies which demonstrate transitional stages between limbic and neocortical structures, and the second concerns investigations of intrahemispheric connections.

Planes of structural development in phylogenesis can also be conceived of as emergent strata. Sanides (1970) has commented that, in the phylogeny of neocortex, "ever new waves of growth and differentiation evolved, and each time a new cortex developed as a core, displacing the previous core to a ringlike structure." In the evolution of neocortex, four principle "growth rings" can be recognized: Periallocortex, proisocortex, parainsular—paralimbic cortex and koniocortex. The classical precentral motor and postcentral somatic regions, which are flanked medially by paralimbic supplementary motor and ventrolaterally by parainsular second sensori—motor area, are preceded in evolution by a stage at which the paralimbic and parainsular representations are contiguous. Moreover, sensori—motor koniocortex, which differentiates out of the preceding paralimbic growth ring, may be a still more recent development than parietal or frontal "integration" cortex, the latter regions serving as a more generalized ground within which the sensori–motor areas appeared.

With regard to cortico–cortical connections there is evidence (Pandya and Kuypers, 1969; Jones and Powell, 1970; Petras, 1971) that frontal "integration" cortex receives projections from the various "sensory" cortices and is in relation to limbic system by way of cingulate gyrus and lateral temporal lobe, and to thalamus by way of nu. dorsomedialis. Similarly, parietal "integration" cortex receives short fiber connections from the "sensory" cortices and is also in relation to limbic system by way of lateral temporal cortex and cingulate gyrus, and to thalamus by way of lateralis posterior and pulvinar. Moreover, there are connections between parietal lobe and frontal granular cortex.

These findings indicate that frontal and parietal "integration" cortices are organized in a similar, if not parallel, fashion. In man, both areas are in relation to "association" cortex surrounding the primary "sensory" areas. Both regions connect to medial and lateral limbic structures and have comparable thalamic representations.

BEHAVIOR

Experimental studies of behavioral change with cortical lesion or stimulation indicate an organization into several modal-specific "sensory" areas and a precentral "motor" zone. The relationship between these "primary" zones and neighboring "secondary" or "association" cortex has been studied chiefly in cases of clinical pathology. Supplementary motor and sensory areas have also been identified in cortex of a more transitional type. In keeping with the more primitive cortex of the supplementary zones, behavior elicited by stimulation of these areas (Penfield and Roberts, 1959) is less well-differentiated (more global, bilateral, and proximal) than that elicited by stimulation of the "primary" neocortical zones.

Studies on visual cortex (Hubel and Wiesel, 1965) suggest the presence of hierarchic stages in the building up of perceptions at the cortical level. Experiments on monkeys (e.g., Weiskrantz, 1968; Pribram, 1958) have demonstrated a differential impairment on discriminative and projective tasks following lesions in the temporal and frontal lobe. Observations on intellection and "language" in chimpanzee (e.g., Gardner and Gardner, 1969; Premack, 1971) indicate a capacity for abstraction (Kluver, 1933) and an ability to produce manual signs or utilize nonsense forms to represent the names of objects or colors (cf. Lenneberg, 1975) that may represent the highest performance at the neocortical stage in subhuman primate.

COGNITION

The various neocortical zones that underlie cognition at this level represent systems through which the final components of cognition are elaborated. Therefore, we may consider visual cortex as a medium for an *endstage* in the perceptual process, not as a simple receptive area. Similarly, motor cortex is neither the site of origin of voluntary movement nor a point *en passage* to other zones, but a final developmental stage in the elaboration of an action.

At the neocortical level, perceptual and action systems show a progressive resolution of both object and action. The perception achieves a delimitation in abstract space and becomes a veridical object; the action undergoes an increasing specification toward a discrete performance with the distal extremity on objects in a space apprehended as real and extrapersonal. The object has been exteriorized and seems to be dissociated from the self. As the object proceeds outward, however, space also becomes more articulated. The object, and the space of the object, "separate" together.

This perceptual development is accompanied by a progression of the action to an asymmetrical motility on exteriorized objects. The action develops with the perception. The graded externalization of the object corresponds to a graded externalization of an action upon that object. The "deception" of the perceived object taken as real has a counterpart in the "deception" of an action on that imagined object.

More highly individuated emotional states emerge with the new perceptual and action forms. Actually, the affect is occasioned by (realized through) these new forms. As the object becomes exteriorized with its space, it draws out or extends from within the range of feeling. The object and its affective component are like arborizations of the affect-ladden image that precedes them.

The perception and the action are accompanied, respectively, by a passive and an active attitude. The passivity of the perceptual process generates a kind of receptiveness to the forming object. This culminates in an eventual "psychic loss" of the object, that is, its detachment as a real or "projected" image in the outer world.

Conversely, the active nature of the action development leads ultimately to a deception of a final exteriorization. The active attitude is also bound up with purposiveness and volition. These conscious states incorporate an affective component.

At this stage, consciousness is that of an object awareness. The object is distinguished from the self, and the self can also be apprehended as an object. An ape can show self-recognition in a mirror. A primitive self-concept is, therefore, possible. This is a self-awareness, however, in which the self is identified as an object; it is another form of object awareness and not a true awareness of self.

The Asymmetric-Symbolic Level

ANATOMY

The phylogenetic trend toward core differentiation discussed in relation to neocortex is continued, in the course of maturation, in the development of cerebral dominance or lateralization. The appearance of new zones of differentiation in frontal and temporo-parietal cortex is the fundamental *structural* achievement at this level. Asymmetry represents a further continuation of this trend. In fact, findings of anatomical asymmetry of the cerebral hemispheres in stillborns (Teszner *et al.*, 1972) can perhaps be interpreted as a first anatomical sign of this evolutionary process thrust into ontogeny. Asymmetry is a prolongation of encephalization into ontogenetic development; it is a solution to the problem of size limitations imposed upon an expanding brain. Hemispheric dominance or lateralization is one expression of this "asymmetrizing" process.

Fundamentally, there is no difference between lateralization and localization; these are different aspects or phases of an unitary process. In fact, lateralization or cerebral dominance is achieved through localization, as a (left) *intrahemispheric* specification for language. Differentiation within the left hemisphere builds up a structure supporting a new cognitive level. At the same time, the realization of this new structural level demands an adaptation (asymmetrization) of earlier bilaterally organized levels. In this way, the acquisition of language acts to transform structure. A model of this asymmetric organization is presented in more detail in the following chapter, in relation to studies of language disorder with brain lesion at different ages and states of laterality.

COGNITION

The designation of this level as "symbolic" conveys more than the usual sense of an idea standing for something; it implies a mode of thought in which "standing for" is understood. The idea is a symbol not when it is simply an idea, but when the idea can be conceptualized qua symbol. The symbol is an attainment beyond the representational. The representation, the act or the perception, takes on a new value.

At this level, cognition achieves a still greater "delay"; the psychological distance between action and perception becomes greater as action and object develop further out of the psychic life. The development proceeds to the point at which action and object seem to be set against cognition as a whole. There is also a progression from purposive to volitional action. Volition, or consciously directed action, is bound up with language development. This is why inaction is also a form of volition; language gives to inaction its voluntary character.

Action has already been exteriorized to a position in extrapersonal space. Speech is a higher form of action and seems to inhabit a different space; this is also true of speech perception. This new space of language develops in the intrapersonal component and not in the extrapersonal field achieved by the previous level. One can say that language permits an articulation of mind in the same way that the world was articulated by objects.

Language development acts also as a vehicle for "consciousness of." The awareness of object—or of self as object—proceeds to an awareness of self as a subject in that awareness. The finer individuation by language of private space carries the awareness development to this further level. Moreover, the awareness experience is closely bound up with affectivity. In fact, awareness is a type of affect. It is the intrapersonal derivation of the affective flow that accompanied the object out into the world. The higher affects—as ideas—are forms of self-valuation deriving from this unitary arborization of affect, awareness, and language together into a new inner or private space.

COMMENT

These four briefly described levels form the basis of a systematic account of the pathology of cognition. Though we must focus on these levels in order to provide a stable framework for a necessarily complicated discussion, the levels may well be little more than arbitrary phases in a continuously unfolding pattern. Such levels have meaning only in so far as they guide our thinking about underlying processes.

The process through which cognition unfolds appears to have the nature of a continuous wave front reiterated at sequential points (levels) in a transitional pattern. In other words, there is a *single* process repeated again and again at successive stages. This concept of an ascending reduplication of a unitary process avoids the problem of a piecemeal construction out of separate partial mechanisms. Each structural level may be thought of as a solution to the problem of carrying an emerging abstract representation through one further transition. The forward direction of the process is maintained by its tendency to unfold, that is, by its transitional nature. The process tends toward a final stage.

The realization of a new performance level will affect cognition at preceding stages. For example, the importance of the hippocampal formation in human memory function has not been definitely confirmed in other animals. This does not reflect a migration of function nor a common physiological organization underlying disparate performances. These differences occur because, in the forward development of cognition, structure acts as a medium for a transformation and is not irrevocably bound to function. As in evolution or embryogenesis, cognition does not advance as an elaboration of the previous endstage. Each new level is not simply a continuation but is a differentiation of an earlier, less specialized stage. One can say that new forms emerge from the depths and not from the varied terminal arborizations. This idea will become clearer in the discussion of lateralization and the neural organization of language. Here we will see that language is not "added on" to prelinguistic cognition, but rather in its development recapitulates all of the preceding stages.

3

Language

My words simply give other people a chance
to remember what they already know.

M. Merleau–Ponty

Language is an *achievement* of cognition. This means that language is not simply added to the human repertoire but is something toward which the organism must strive. In the same sense, the words in an utterance are not the building blocks of that utterance, but are the final aim toward which that utterance is directed. It is to this prehistory of the utterance that Vygotsky (1970) referred when he wrote, "A word is a microcosm of human consciousness."

Speech is one form of action through which language is realized. It is different from other forms of action in that the object of the action has become quite removed from the action itself. Speech has as its object a content in speech perception. This content undergoes a development parallel to that of speech, however widely separated the perception and the speech act may appear. In speech, the effectuation upon the (distant)

25

object becomes highly abstract. It is in this way that wholly artificial symbols objectify and come to be taken for existents in "extrapersonal" space. A central point is that no matter how highly differentiated their endproducts, both speech and speech perception differentiate out of the same deep organization.

As a form of action, speech formation occurs over a series of levels leading from somatic to extrasomatic space. There is also a progression from an object bond to "purposive" action (speech) where the psychological *distance* of the object is sufficiently great as to suggest a direction toward a goal. In language this progression is enhanced, so that the more widely separated speech act and object (speech perception) give the impression of a decision-like operation. In this way, language carries the developing volitional attitude one stage further than pure motility. The inner bond between volition and language is a central feature of all forms of language pathology.

Language develops through a formative or microgenetic process as one of several components of cognition. In this development, the content passes from one stage to another, though generally we apprehend only the final products and are not aware of the developmental process itself. These earlier, otherwise concealed (i.e., traversed) levels, however, reveal themselves when they appear as pathological speech forms. When this occurs during sleep or with fatigue or medication, it is a transient phenomenon. Language of this type may be hard to study and is usually taken as a simple aberration of the normal mechanism. Even in profound psychosis, an abnormal speech form may not persist. With structural brain lesion, however, the earlier stage, the aphasic syndrome, can become a final speech product and may persist indefinitely as a relatively stable form. Pathological language of this type affords an opportunity to study, at a leisurely pace, the psychological determinants of normal utterances.

Every abnormal utterance has a lawful pattern, and the laws of pathology are the same as those of normal function. Every pathological speech form or aphasia can be conceived as a preliminary level in normal language that pathology has brought to the fore. At each such level, the aphasia also points to a corresponding stage in cognitive development. Thus, we may study an aphasia both from the point of view of language, as a manifestation of a prefigurative stage in the normal process, and from the point of view of cognition, as exhibiting features characteristic of whatever cognitive stage happens to be realized in the momentary level. With this in mind, we may proceed to a discussion of the organization of language as revealed by a study of pathological cases.

THE POSTERIOR SYSTEM

The posterior disorders of language fall into three major linguistic categories, the semantic, the nominal, and the phonemic (see Figure 2a). These represent disruptions at, respectively, the limbic-presentational, cortical-representational, and asymmetric-symbolic stages of the described cognitive hierarchy. These aphasias also refer to stages in the sequence of normal language production. This sequence unfolds on an axis between a semantic or selectional process and a stage of phonemic encoding. The precursors of the words, the forms or clusters of the utterance to be, emerge through a semantic operation by means of which the developing utterance is shaped in the direction of the final performance. At this stage, there appears to be a "noun priority" in the entry of lexical items into the forming sentence pattern. A transition then occurs from the ordered abstract sentence frame to the phonemic representatives of the constituent words in preparation for articulation. At this stage, the small (function) words are introduced. In the course of this process, both a referential (i.e., nominative) and an expositional (i.e., discursive) orientation can be discerned, a distinction which has helped to clarify some of the complex interrelationships between these forms.

As has been discussed earlier, every disorder of language also incorporates aspects of a corresponding level in cognition. A change in awareness, an alteration of mood, the presence or absence of delusional or hallucinatory phenomena, these are not additions to the clinical picture but have an inner bond with the aphasic form.

Phonemic $\left\{\begin{array}{l}\text{phonemic (conduction) aphasia}\\[4pt]\text{phonemic paraphasia}\end{array}\right.$

Nominal $\left\{\begin{array}{l}\text{anomia}\\\text{circumlocution}\\\text{verbal paraphasia}\end{array}\right.$

Semantic $\left\{\begin{array}{l}\text{semantic aphasia}\\\text{semantic paraphasia}\\\text{semantic jargon}\end{array}\right.$

Levels	*Referential defect*	*Expositional defect*	*Combined defect*
Phonemic ↑	Phonemic errors in naming and repetition, with good conversational speech.	Phonemic errors in conversational speech, with good naming and repetition.	Phonemic aphasia, errors in naming, repetition and conversation.
Nominal ↑	Impaired word-finding on naming tests and good conversational speech.	"Empty" conversational speech, with good naming.	Nominal aphasia, impaired word-finding in speech and on naming tests.
Semantic	Word substitution on naming ("associative" to "categorical" errors) with good conversational speech.	Derailments in conversational speech, with good naming.	Semantic jargon, ("associative" to "asemantic" errors) in speech and naming.

FIGURE 2. (*a*). Sequence and pattern of impairment in posterior aphasia. (*b*). Specific disturbances in referential and/or expositional speech at sequential levels in language production.

SEMANTIC DISORDERS

The various states of pathological language pointing to a disruption at the semantic level can be described with respect to three different language forms; one or more of these elements is apparent in every disorder that can be referred to this stage. Semantic jargon is, in some respects, the most pronounced of these forms, while semantic aphasia and semantic paraphasia may be considered as partial forms.

Semantic Jargon

This phenomenon is basically a disorder of word meaning that involves both naming and conversational speech in the presence of moderate loss of oral comprehension. In organic cases, there is generally a lesion of the posterior middle and superior temporal gyrus (posterior T2 and T1), often bilaterally. In older patients, the lesion is more commonly unilateral and on the left side.

Semantic jargon is one form of Wernicke's ("receptive," "sensory") aphasia. Such patients produce good words and sentences, but there is defective meaning. An example is a patient who described a *fork* as "a need for a schedule" (Alajouanine, 1952), or another who defined a *spoon* as "How many schemes on your throat." Another patient, asked about his poor vision, said, "My wires don't hire right." A case of Kreindler *et al.* (1971) replied to a question about his health with: "I felt worse because I can no longer keep in mind from the mind of the minds to keep me from mind and up to the ear which can be to find among ourselves." A patient of Heilbronner responded to a similar question with "Yes, I think that I am now so safe than now much with others to some extent directly." Occasionally, neologisms are present which may lead to strinkingly bizarre utterances. Thus, an aphasic physician, asked if he was a doctor, said "Me? yes sir. I'm a male demaploze on my own. I still know my tubaboys what for I have that's gone hell and some of them go."

Speech production is fluent; there is no word search despite the incorrect choices, and vocabulary use is fairly good, at times even pretentious. There is semantic or verbal paraphasia on tests of naming and repetition. By this is meant a substitution of one word for another, for example, "table" for chair. In semantic jargon, however, the link between the substitution and the target word is often not as clear as in the "in-class" substitution of this example. Rather, a patient might call a chair an "engine" or an "Argentina." The term semantic paraphasia can be used for this latter type of substitution, and verbal paraphasia for categorical substitution.

Comprehension is moderately impaired, though ordinarily some understanding is possible, while reading aloud and writing show alterations parallel to those of speech. There is commonly a euphoric, at times manic, mood elevation or aggressiveness. Paranoia and auditory hallucinations may occur. Patients tend to be logorrheic, and they show partial or complete absence of awareness for their defective speech. However, they will usually reject jargon spoken by the examiner and will resist efforts to correct their own speech. The awareness of speech content, as with all other elements of the syndrome, may change from moment to moment. Awareness appears to be inversely related to the semantic "distance" of the utterance from its presumed goal.

In deeply regressed schizophrenic patients, speech very similar to semantic jargon—so-called word salad (the *Wortsalat* of Bleuler)—may occur. Some examples are: "We are already standing in the spiral under a hammer" (Kraepelin, 1919); "The house burnt the cow horrendendously (sic) always" (Arieti, 1975); "A priest doll and a tree are part of the close by Sunday school not at that location now" (personal case). Nowadays, with the medication that is available, it is unusual to see schizophasic speech of this type, but there is no question but that it occurs, that it is part of the schizophrenic syndrome and does not represent a misdiagnosed organic aphasia.

This stage of unintelligible semantic jargon may resolve in one of two directions; to involvement of expositional speech with intact naming, or involvement of referential speech (naming) with preserved conversation. The former is termed *semantic aphasia*, the latter (pure) *semantic paraphasia*. Both of these disorders occur with bilateral temporal lobe pathology.

Semantic Aphasia

This disorder was first described as an interruption at a prelinguistic phase in the thought–speech transition (Head, 1926). Patients demonstrated a lack of recognition of the full significance of words and phrases apart from their verbal meaning. There was a failure to comprehend the final aim or goal of an action and inability to clearly formulate a general conception of what was heard, read, or seen in a picture, although many of the details were enumerated.

More recent studies show that, in semantic aphasia, there is a disturbance of contextual meaning through which utterances of "skewed meaning" are produced. The disorder is especially prominent with proverb, story, or picture interpretation. Consider this example of a patient's written description of his speech (patient's capitals and punctuation).

> Speech that could be found as a Type of speed I believe. I possible mood of my own maybe because of misunderstanding. Possibly because of my own thought in a certain way. a friend of mine told myself. I had a "cast Iron Fact" especially during a conversation.

The disorder is apparent in both speech and writing; speech is fluent and somewhat logorrheic and may have a confabulatory flavor. Comprehension may be quite good, while naming, reading aloud, and repetition are intact. Spatial-constructional difficulty may or may not be present; and the neurological examination can be normal except for the aphasia. Patients tend to be euphoric with only partial insight into their disability. Paranoia and hallucination are not prominent features, but insufficient cases have been described for one to be certain of this.

In the above example of aphasic speech, we also see features commonly identified with schizophrenic utterance, such as increased self-reference, unusual expressions, and ellipse; there is even the tendency in writing, described in some schizophrenics, to capitalize words within the sentence. In fact, semantic aphasia represents a disorder intermediate between the more clearly demarcated thought (psychotic) and language (aphasic) impairments. For this reason, it helps to reveal the weakness of the distinction based on alteration (e.g., substitution) in either thought or language, for example, paralogia versus paraphasia (Kleist, 1960; Schneider, 1925), a distinction that breaks down in the face of a demonstration of a whole graduated series of transitions between the thought and language disorders. If the schizophrenic does not show typical anomic, syntactical, or paraphasic symptoms, this is because his defect is at a stage at which language is more "thought like." Rumke and Nijdam (1958) have even asked if it is "possible to conceive a genuine delusion, as regards its form, as an extremely "high-level" aphasic impairment." Certainly, aphasic patients with semantic jargon may show delusional thinking, just as schizophrenics with delusion can show semantic jargon. The resolution of this problem depends on whether thought is viewed as something external or prior to language or as an earlier stage in language, that is, as language at a greater degree of depth.

Examples of intermediate language of the semantic aphasic type are found outside of schizophrenia and the aphasias. Thus, Korsakoff patients have been described with a type of paralogia in the verbal sphere, as the patient of Clarke *et al.* (1958) who replied to the proverb *Safety First*: "It's rather a lateral term which means it could apply to a host of things. A road for one thing." Compare this to the schizophrenic described by Woods (1938) who responded to the proverb *Let Sleeping Dogs Lie*, with: "It would be normal to any object that was seemingly comfortable to let it remain uncomfortable and if there was something to be appreciably gained it would be better to let it continue." Such utterances are probably identical to the *"confabulation d'origine verbale"* of Pfersdorff (1935) noted in catatonics. This form of confabulation is said to differ from that of Korsakoff patients in the decisive influence of the word, but there is little evidence one way or another on this point. In all such patients, however, whether schizophrenic, aphasic, Korsakovian, presbyophrenic, or confused, the common element is a preservation of the general meaning or direction of the utterance, and its syntax, and an associative or elliptical quality to the expression by means of which this meaning is achieved. Moreover, such patients also show incomplete awareness of error and poor self-correction, impaired speech comprehension to some degree, and or-nateness and mannerism in word use. Kraepelin also noted these similari-ties, as well as the fluency, euphoria, and playful (ludic) speech quality.

Finally, similar utterances may be found in transitional states, for example, "They are exposed to verbally interlection" (Froeschels, 1946), and in normal sleeptalking, for example, "You kept bouncing them on and on as if you had a regular meter . . ." (Arkin and Brown, 1971).

Semantic Paraphasia

In this disorder which has (incorrectly) been termed "non-aphasic misnaming" (Weinstein and Keller, 1964), conversational speech is fairly well-preserved, but errors occur on tests of object naming. These take the form of "associative" responses, for example, a *pipe* is called a "smoker," *glasses* a "telescope." The pretentious and facetious quality of the paraphasia appears in such instances as when a *doctor* is called a "butcher" or a *syringe* a "hydrometer to measure fluids." The paraphasia affects about 10%–15% of names produced, depending upon test item. Although the object naming difficulty may follow a word-frequency distribution, this does not hold true for the paraphasic response.

The disorder usually occurs in the context of diffuse disease, drowsiness, or confusion. Speech is fluent, at times logorrheic, but not clearly aphasic. Comprehension is good, and repetition is preserved. Patients show euphoria, reduced speech awareness, and/or denial.

Schizophrenic patients may show misnaming of this type, as in Goldstein's (1943) example of the patient who said "le song" for bird, and "kiss" for mouth. Victor (1972) has noted word-finding difficulty and misnaming in acute Korsakoff patients. In my experience, this more commonly takes the form of semantic paraphasia than of categorical substitution. In fact, there appears to be an inner relationship between confabulation and this type of paraphasia. Thus, as in the patient of Victor *et al.* (1971) who, when asked his name, replied "Herman Joseph Prince Macaroni," misnaming may occur as a performance transitional to frank confabulation.

Mechanism of the Semantic Disorders

Three disorders of semantic origin have been described:

1. *semantic aphasia* when context (expositional speech) is primarily affected
2. *semantic paraphasia* with disturbance in referential speech
3. *semantic jargon* when both reference and context are involved.

The fact that the first and second forms occur independently indicates that one is not a partial expression of the other, though semantic jargon may be taken as a combination of the two. The mechanism that accounts for the disorder is similar in both the expositional and referential forms. In *semantic aphasia* the speaker is unable to use the verb or predicate of the forming utterance as a free unit to which the subject and object only partially relate. A combination of any two of these elements (e.g., subject and verb, or verb and object) tends to determine the third. The direction is not invariably subject → verb → object but is often the reverse. All lexical items may be affected, and it may be difficult to determine which element of the phrase is defective. In the aforementioned example, "speech that could be found . . . ," acceptable bondings occur between individual words (speech that, that could, could be found) but not between the initial and latter segments of the phrase. As mentioned earlier, the disorder has a close relation to schizophrenic speech. Consider an example from the study of paralogic by von Domarus:

$$\text{Certain Indians } (A) \text{ / are / swift } (x)$$
$$\text{Stags} \qquad (B) \text{ / are / swift } (x)$$
$$\text{Certain Indians } (A) \text{ are stags } (B)$$

$$\text{Here, } A \cong x \text{ becomes } A = x$$
$$B \cong x \text{ becomes } B = x$$
$$A \cong x \cong B < \quad \text{becomes } A = x = B$$

This is quite similar to what occurs in semantic aphasia. Thus, in the following example from a "Cloze" test, an aphasic patient was required to insert words where deleted from a test phrase. The patient's solution is in brackets. The test phrase is "The baby—something that he had—done before."

A	x	B
The baby	[was]	something
that he had	[been]	done before

$$\text{Here, } A \cong x \text{ and } \quad x \cong B \text{ becomes } A = B$$

The inserted word agrees with those in its immediate surroundings (e.g., baby *was, was* something; had *been, been* done), and a partial fit is accepted as satisfactory. Responses to proverb tests show identical errors; the patients generally interpret one component of the proverb partially and then attempt to consolidate it obliquely with the other components.

In *semantic aphasia,* the noun phrase tends to become stabilized at the expense of its predicative relationships. Context is adapted to subject. One might say that the noun phrase conditions the predicate. This has a determining effect upon utterances in which topics are developed within understood contexts. In *semantic paraphasia* (see example), misnamings show the influence of implicit contexts derived from the examiner's knowledge of the object to be named. Predicative or contextual function, however, is otherwise adequate and acts to normalize noun production in conversational speech.

In *semantic paraphasia,* there is an identification of two otherwise disparate subjects (e.g., "doctor" and "butcher") on the basis of one or two shared attributes (e.g., white coat, cutting, etc.). Consider this example:

Task	Presented Object A	Shared Predicate C	Paraphasic Response B
naming	bedpan	stool, sitting, etc.	"piano stool"

$$Mechanism$$
$$A \cong C$$
$$B \cong C$$
$$A = B$$

Comment

These three constituents of the semantic level of pathology are not stable entities. Rather there is in many patients, whether organic or functional, a constant fluctuation from one form to another. Moreover, in cases both of the organic and the functional series, an *inner* relationship is evident between the momentary speech form and the affective–cognitive matrix within which the form appears. The paranoia or mania of the organic does not differ intrinsically from that of the functional case. The lack of awareness of the defective utterance, the auditory inattentiveness, and the "replacement" by auditory hallucination of the speech perceptive field are common elements in both groups. Similarly, semantic errors appearing in normal individuals, for example, during sleeptalking (Arkin and Brown, 1971), hypnagogy, or distraction, though not studied from the point of view of affective relationships do show, for the specific utterance, a greater lack of content awareness than occurs with errors of the anomic or phonemic type (q.v.).

NOMINAL DISORDERS

The developing linguistic form, having more or less successfully traversed the semantic or selectional stage, proceeds toward the "abstract representation" of the (correct) lexical item. Disorders at this level will, therefore, be characterized by improved control of word meaning but also by an inability to evoke the intended word. As with the preceding stage, anomia (difficulty in finding words) is not a single entity but is, rather, a series of (pathological) speech forms that point to one or another segment or phase of the process of language production. A disturbance at this stage may occur, to some extent, independently in referential speech (as in anomia proper, word-finding difficulty) and in expositional speech (so-called "empty speech" of anomia, circumlocution). Verbal paraphasia occurs as well and is to be distinguished from semantic ("asemantic") paraphasia, as defined earlier, on the basis of the "in-class" nature of the substitution ("shaver" for razor, "green" for red). Verbal paraphasia is to be seen as an intermediate stage between semantic paraphasia and anomia proper.

Verbal Paraphasia

This disorder refers to a stage at which the lexical item, the word, has realized (been selected to the point of) a categorical approximation, for example, "shaver" for razor, "green" for red. There is some ability to self-correct, that is, some awareness of speech error, but this may differ from one moment to the next depending on the nature of the substitution. Although the difficulty in naming may have a relation to the vocabulary frequency of the target word (i.e., patients having more difficulty with rare than with common words), the paraphasic errors do not show this effect. Thus, patients may say "spectacles" for glasses, or "fuchsia" for red. While this form of language is often admixed with other anomic features (vide infra), the absence of verbal paraphasia in anomia proper should not be interpreted as a reluctance to speak or as evidence of a more careful search for words. Verbal paraphasia is not a reflection of personality type; rather, it reflects a cognitive level around which the "personality" is organized. Features of this cognitive level include some degree of euphoria, a more active though not logorrheic speech flow than in anomia, and partial awareness of the disorder.

Anomic Aphasia (Anomia, Amnesic, or Nominal Aphasia)

Patients of this type have difficulty in word finding that affects nouns preferentially. Typically, such patients can point to the correct object when it is named for them, can repeat the object name, and can select the correct name from a group, although they are unable to name the object directly. This is true for "visual naming" as well as naming through other perceptual modes, such as touching the object, hearing the sound of the object, and so on. In addition, patients cannot name from a description or definition of the object: for example, "What do you use to sweep the floor?" The word-finding difficulty may be akin to the common phenomenon of word lapse or of forgetting a name or place in the speech flow. The incipient, "tip-of-the-tongue" nature of the demanded word is not uncommon. Patients may be able to give the initial letter of the target word or the number of syllables and can use the test object appropriately. These features suggest that word meaning is relative well-preserved and that some "skeleton" or abstract frame of the intended word is available. The disorder may be limited to referential speech, or it may appear in conversation with circumlocution and emptiness of speech. The true anomic who does not produce verbal paraphasias has a more acute awareness of his difficulty and may show frustration and catastrophic reactions.

The difficulty in word finding tends to occur in the following direction: nouns→verbs→grammatical (function) words. Abstract nouns may be more difficult than concrete nouns. When the disorder involves both referential and expositional speech, a "nonfluent" state can result. Such patients will have greatly reduced speech with only a phrase or a stereotypy available, such as "Well I . . ." or "It's a . . . ." Speech tends to be limited to small grammatical words and simple verbs.

Word-finding difficulty occurs in various organic and nonorganic states. Anomia and circumlocution have been described in schizophrenia. Chapman and Chapman (1973) have emphasized that schizophrenic patients "have a true difficulty in word finding, although it tends to be episodic in occurrence and very similar to the paroxysmal dysgraphia which occurs in temporal lobe epilepsy." Anomic errors are also common in fatigue, distraction, and in sleep and transitional utterance.

Anomia tends to be associated with either unilateral or diffuse lesions. In anomia and in verbal paraphasia, lesions may occur outside the classical speech areas. The more severe "nonfluent" anomia occurs with unilateral (left) temporo-parietal lesion. Lesions of the posterior middle temporal gyrus (T2) and its continuation to angular gyrus appear to be highly correlated with this form. The more fluent the anomia is, the more likely is diffuse pathology or lesion outside the speech area.

COMMENT ON THE SEMANTIC AND NOMINAL DISORDERS

The various disorders that have been discussed thus far can be arranged in a series that retraces the microgenetic development of normal language. The sequence of semantic jargon, through associative and then categorical substitution to true anomia, corresponds to stages in the normal productive process. Within the semantic "segment," the progression is through systems or fields of word meaning of "wide psychological distance." These lead to more narrow "associative" responses that represent an intermediate stage between semantic jargon and correct word selection. Anomia points to a stage at which the correct word has been all but selected but cannot yet be fully realized in speech. The anomic stage corresponds to

the emergence of the correct lexical item preparatory to phonemic encoding.

In addition to this linguistic change, there is an evolution of other aspects of cognition. Thus, in semantic jargon there is euphoria, at times mania, often with a paranoid trend. There is logorrhea and a lack of awareness of speech error. This picture gives way in semantic aphasia and semantic paraphasia to a mitigation of logorrhea and euphoria with patchy but still incomplete awareness of difficulty. This continues into verbal paraphasia, where incorrect words (e.g., "table" for chair) can often be rejected. There is a transition from active, but not logorrheic, speech to hesitancy, and finally to a near inability to speak at all. The transition from one state to another occurs pari passu with increasing awareness of speech errors, improved self-correction, and step-by-step transformation from one affective and behavioral form to another.

PHONEMIC DISORDERS

These disorders point to a stage in the production of language at which the intended word, although it has been properly selected, does not achieve correct phonemic realization. According to whether the defect is expressed primarily in referential or in expositional speech, we can distinguish, respectively, phonemic paraphasia and phonemic aphasia. Ordinarily, these are included together in the syndrome of central or conduction aphasia.

Phonemic Paraphasia

In this disorder, the disturbance primarily affects the content words and is apparent on tests of object naming and repetition. Spontaneous or conversational speech may be quite good with few or rare paraphasias. Patients make errors of the type: "predident" for president. The use of nonsense words on repetition tests helps to bring out the disorder more clearly. Comprehension is often quite good. Such patients are usually classified as either mild "conduction" aphasics or mild motor aphasics. In fact, the intermediate position of phonemic paraphasia (as opposed to phonemic aphasia, see later) points to an endstage convergence of both the anterior and posterior systems at the phonemic–articulatory level.

Phonemic Aphasia (Central, Conduction Aphasia)

When conversational speech shows a picture of fluent phonemic paraphasia with phonemic errors on naming and repetition tasks and good comprehension, the diagnosis of phonemic aphasia is in order. There is a close resemblance to phonemic paraphasia; the distinction rests on the improved speech and defective naming and repetition of the former, and the more impaired spontaneous speech of the latter, where naming may be relatively well-preserved and repetition is involved at the phrase, rather than single-word, level. This disorder may be present at the start, may appear in the course of a deteriorating anomia, and as a stage in the recovery of neologistic jargon (vide infra). An example of such speech is that of a patient who, when asked where she lived, said: "I have been spa staying with a friend of mine but I do hate to imp impose on her. I want to pay my own way. Do they have some sort of chart where you can take this tee tee. . . ." When phonemic aphasia develops out of neologistic jargon (q.v.), speech is more active with some neologism and comprehension is less well-preserved. Such a patient described his speech difficulty as: "Well it's very hard to because I don't know what it would my pi why what's wrong with it, but I can't food, it's food and rood to read the way I used to do all right off . . . ."

The disturbance is equally present in naming and repetition and in a manner generally comparable to conversational speech. This is particularly evident when phonemic aphasia appears in the deterioration of an anomia. Thus, if an anomic patient is asked to name an ashtray, the word is not produced, but it can be repeated. In the regression of the anomia, the patient will first fail to cue with the initial sound of the word, that is, when the examiner says "ash . . . ," but will still repeat the word "ashtray." At a later stage, failure will occur in spite of a strong phonemic cue, for example, "ashtr . . . ," in which all but the final syllable of the word is given, but the word "ashtray" can still be repeated. Ultimately, a stage is reached at which the patient can neither cue nor repeat. At this point, the patient is a phonemic (conduction) aphasic (Brown, 1975). In this example, we can see that the *disorder of repetition is only a failure to name given the whole word as a cue.* The transition from the anomic, who repeats the word but fails to name with a cue up to the penultimate syllable, to the *phonemic aphasic,* who fails when given a cue including the final syllable (i.e., on repetition), establishes a functional continuity between these two disorders. There is a different speech form in these patients since the phonemic aphasic has achieved a linguistic level beyond that of the anomic. There is also a heightened awareness of speech content. Circumlocution has given way to deficient production, frustration to self-correction.

With regard to anatomical correlation, the evidence suggests that dominant posterior-superior temporal gyrus and its "parietal continuation" as supramarginal gyrus are chiefly involved. Cases with a lesion of angular gyrus have been reported, as well as instances in younger patients with a lesion limited to the left Wernicke's area.

Phonemic aphasia is uncommon in nonorganic states, but phonemic errors may occur in speech during fatigue or distraction. An example of such errors in normal sleep-talking is the following: "David, I day [say?] David . . . that's you that day dated day dravid Dave dravid about 25 or 30 noked naked day dreams" (Arkin & Brown, 1971). The "clang association" is more prominent than is generally seen in phonemic aphasia, although clang errors are prominent in neologistic jargon (vide infra).

THE PROBLEM OF NEOLOGISM

Aphasic jargon with neologism is a disturbance altogether different from semantic jargon, although both disorders are often treated as different manifestations of Wernicke's aphasia. As in the semantic, nominal, and phonemic disorders, there may be two expressions of the defect, in referential speech, as neologistic paraphasia, and in both referential and expositional speech, as neologistic jargon.

Neologistic Paraphasia

In this disorder, speech is generally comprehensible with occasional neologism, often in the context of fluent phonemic paraphasia. The neologism appears especially when a highly specific response is demanded, such as on proverb interpretation and under the conditions of naming. An example is the following, from a patient who was questioned about his work: "[I]t was my job as a convince, a confoser, not confoler but almost the same as a man who was commersed." Another patient described her accident in the following way: "So when I passed drive I told him let me drive. I had go so he let me go, so I went, wen in and went in on the semidore." The neologism primarily affects content words, with the small grammatical words relatively spared. The disorder is probably closely allied to phonemic aphasia and paraphasia; the neologism at times appears as a phonemic error severe enough to render the word unintelligible (see also Lecours, 1974).

Neologistic Jargon

This disorder refers to speech so involved with neologism that it is no longer intelligible. The neologisms may range from word-like products to a series of clang contaminations. Thus, one patient responded to the idiom "swell headed" with the interpretation "She is selfice on purpiten," while, at another time, when asked about her speech problem, she said: "Because no one gotta scotta gowan thwa thirst gell gerst derund gystrol that's all." A progression may be seen from fluent, logorrheic neologistic speech with few clang associations, to reiteration of certain neologisms and perseverations on the basis of sound similarity to clang association that is so intense that it seems to determine the jargon output, for example: "Then he graf, so I'll graf, I'm giving ink, no, gefergen, in pane, I can't grasp, I haven't grob the grabben, I'm going to the glimmeril let me go."

In such patients, comprehension is densely impaired. Naming and repetition are characterized by neologistic responses, such as "galeefs" for comb, "errendear" for yellow. There is a lack of awareness of speech errors, and patients will gesture actively, seemingly convinced that they are communicating something to the examiner. There is heightened affectivity, often with euphoria and exaggerated expression. It is interesting that patients will appear to accept their own jargon if it is recorded and played back to them, but they will reject the same (transcribed) jargon if it is spoken to them by an examiner.

The pathological location of the lesion is in dominant posterior-superior temporal region. There is evidence that the lesion incorporates both Wernicke's area proper and supramarginal gyrus.

In schizophrenia, neologisms are more often of the "portmanteau" type; they are either fusions of separate words (e.g., mondteufel, cage-weather juice, snowhousehold) or assimilations of otherwise recognizable components of separate words (e.g., enduration for *endure* plus *concentration*). These forms can perhaps be explained along the lines suggested for semantic paraphasia (q.v.). Occasionally, unintelligible utterances may occur, such as: "I have seen you but your words alworthen" (What does alworthen mean?); "Ashers guiding the circumfrax" (see Bleuler, 1950, for other examples). In schizophasic jargon, one may encounter utterances of the type: "Ulrass Asia peru arull pelhuss Pisa anuell pelli." Similar types of jargon may be seen in transitional states, for example, "amarande es tifiercia" (Froeschels, 1946) and in sleep speech, for example, "she shad hero sher sher sheril shaw takes part . . ." (Arkin and Brown, 1971). A form of aphasic jargon referred to as undifferentiated or phonemic jargon may resemble such utterances as "Eh oh malaty, eh favility, abelabla tay kate abelabla tay to po sta here, aberda yeste day [yesterday ?]."

Interpretation of Neologistic Jargon

Although the position of neologistic jargon in the aphasias is uncertain, there is evidence that, at least in the most florid cases, it may represent a combination of semantic jargon and phonemic aphasia. In such cases, semantic paraphasias would be produced that would not achieve correct phonemic realization, the result being a phonemic distortion superimposed on a semantic paraphasia. This is consistent with the fact that neologistic jargon tends to improve to either semantic jargon or phonemic aphasia. Thus, if the semantic disorder clears, the patient is left with a phonemic defect, while clearing of the phonemic disorder would reveal the underlying semantic disturbance. In other (milder) cases, however, the neologism probably consists of a normal underlying word frame that is distorted to the point of unintelligibility by phonemic paraphasia. In addition, there are certainly many instances, as was illustrated earlier, in which the neologism is a result of clang associations and/or word fusions.

Comment

The process of language production has been traced through several stages, from a level of semantic encoding through a phase of word selection to one of phonemic realization. Moreover, a transitional infrastructure has been shown between the semantic and nominal levels, and between the nominal and phonemic levels.

The semantic disorders tend to occur with bilateral temporal lobe pathology. This is especially true of younger patients. Anomia is more strongly associated with left-sided lesions, but it involves a wider extent of neocortex than the phonemic disorders, which are related to more specific left (dominant) hemispheric lesions. Neologistic jargon, by reason of its dependence on a constituent of phonemic aphasia (neologistic jargon appears to be phonemic aphasia that has deteriorated, or with semantic jargon) is also bound to focal left hemisphere pathology.

The deeper the disorder is in the hierarchy, the greater is the tendency for bilateral lesion. The more superficial the disorder is, the greater is the tendency for unilateral (dominant hemisphere) lesion. Moreover, the bilateral lesions of the earlier level disturbances, for example those of semantic jargon, may well not involve true neocortex, but rather the *cortical representatives of limbic structures.* In anomia, neocortex is involved more generally, while in phonemic aphasia, the lesion concerns the most asymmetrically organized portion of neocortex. Thus, the microgenetic levels to which each pathological form corresponds also have a relation to structural systems identified with those microgenetic levels.

The final abstract form of the posterior series, that of the phonemic realization of the utterance to be, is not simply conveyed forward for articulation. Rather there is, corresponding to the posterior series of levels, an anterior series of speech forms centered about the action component of cognition. The posterior linguistic and anterior action components unfold together into the final *language act*. One might say that these regions are organized in a parallel, not sequential, fashion.

THE ANTERIOR SYSTEM

In a manner similar to that of the posterior disorders, pathology of the anterior speech zone uncovers a series of stages in action formation leading from deep to superficial levels. A progression can be observed (Figure 3) from akinetic mutism, through mutism without akinesia, to transcortical motor aphasia, which is a kind of selective mutism, through agrammatism to Broca's or anarthric aphasia. Each of these disorders involves an ascending stage in cognition, and the associated pathological lesion involves an increasingly more asymmetric substrate.

MUTISM

The classical akinetic mute state that follows disruption at the sensori—motor level gives way at the limbic stage to a partial form with a more pronounced affective element. There may be a dissociation between facio—vocal and body motility; the occurrence of agitated and aggressive episodes during the otherwise mute state is also characteristic. This occurs in both functional and organic disorders. On the one hand, mutism, with or without akinesis, is observed in regressed schizophrenic patients, as in the "drive-poor" catatonia of Kleist, or psychotic stupor, and in the cyclical motility paralyses. Alternation or coexistance of akinesis with manic display is common. The picture is similar to that of bilateral lesion of cingulate gyrus (e.g., cases of Nielsen, 1951; Buge *et al.*, 1975). Mutism tends to occur with considerable alertness and often without somatic akinesia.

Placidity, rather than mutism, follows surgical cingulotomy. This is presumably a partial expression of the more severe akinesis of larger lesions, and it reveals the affective element present even in profound akinetic states. Following surgical section of the forebrain commisures, most patients have mutism unaccompanied by akinesia for several weeks

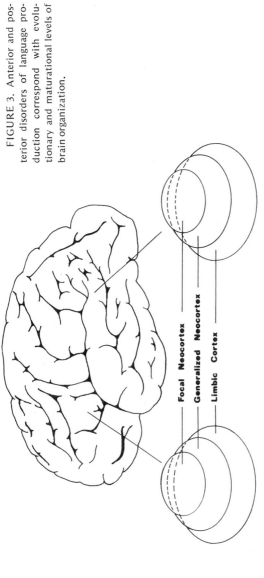

FIGURE 3. Anterior and posterior disorders of language production correspond with evolutionary and maturational levels of brain organization.

Focal Neocortex
Generalized Neocortex
Limbic Cortex

Anterior (nonfluent) aphasia

Phonemic-articulatory disorder (anarthric aphasia)

Agrammatism

Mutism with or without akinesis

Structural level

Specialized Neocortex
Left focal lesion

Generalized Neocortex
Partial or peripheral lesion of speech zone on left side

Limbic Cortex
Bilateral or unilateral lesion

Posterior (fluent) aphasia

Phonemic aphasia

Nominal aphasia

Semantic aphasia

(Bogen, 1972). Such patients recover through a stage of hoarseness without dysarthria or aphasia. Mutism is a late stage in the Marchiafava– Bignami disease, where there is necrosis of the corpus callosum, as well as in some cases of callosal tumor. The mechanism here, as in callosotomy, is probably involvement of underlying cingulate fibers. In these cases, agitated or frankly psychotic behavior is common.

Mutism is not uncommon in acute aphasia. This has been attributed to diaschisis, to widespread ischemia, or to minor hemisphere suppression. It is probable that, in such cases, the mutism reflects the bilateral effects of an otherwise unilateral lesion. This phenomenon has been observed in thalamic lesion, where the picture of an *acute* unilateral (left-sided) lesion, that is, mutism, resembles the endstage of progressive bilateral pathology (Brown, 1974). In aphasic patients with initial speech loss, there is usually a paucity of nonspeech vocalization as well as a loss of comprehension. After a few days or weeks, the condition tends to improve into one of the partial aphasias. In young children, mutism is the most common expression of acquired aphasia and may result from lesions throughout the (dominant) hemisphere. Prolonged mutism may also occur as an aphasic symptom in "anomalous" dextrals (aphasic dextrals with a right hemisphere lesion) and may be more common in left-handed aphasics regardless of lesion lateralization.

These various disorders point to a disruption of vocalization at a limbic level within the emerging action component. This occurs with a lesion of bilateral limbic structures or transitional cortex. Possibly extensive neocortical involvement can also produce a regression to a limbic structural stage.

TRANSCORTICAL MOTOR APHASIA

The *transition* from the limbic to the neocortical level is marked by the progression of cingulate mutism to transcortical motor aphasia. This condition is characterized by a marked poverty of speech, and occasionally by slowness of movement (bradykinesia), but with good repetition. Nonspeech vocalization may also be reduced. Comprehension of speech is ordinarily good, and naming is usually accurate within the limits of available speech. According to Goldstein (1948), there are two forms of the disorder: a transient type characterized by good repetition, impaired series speech, and agrammatism, due to a "heightening of the speech threshold," and a more typical variety described earlier that involves loss of the "speech impulse" (see Brown, 1972).

The usual anatomical correlation is with lesions of dominant middle frontal gyrus or partial involvement of Broca's area. This may not be completely accurate, however, since the most common etiology, occlusion of anterior cerebral artery, also entails damage to cingulate gyrus and neighboring paralimbic and supplementary motor cortices.

In this regard, vocalization resembling sounds emitted by a monkey has been produced by stimulation of the anterior portion of the cingulate gyrus in both monkey and dog (Kaada, 1960). The vocalization is elicited from the medial surface only in an area limited to the upper forward portion of the anterior cingulate region and the banks of the cingulate gyrus. In man, vocalization of a similar type, as well as speech perseveration, have been produced by stimulation or lesion of the supplementary motor area lying just above cingulate gyrus. This latter area has been shown to be a paralimbic expansion zone of encephalized limbic cortex (Sanides, 1970) and intermediate in type between the latter and neocortex. The supplementary motor area and related paralimbic structures derived from, and possibly including, the cingulate portion of limbic system may be the anatomical correlates of transcortical motor aphasia. If so, the syndrome can be considered a type of partial mutism, transitional between mutism without akinesia occurring with bilateral involvement of cingulate gyrus, and the selective speech loss, Broca's aphasia and agrammatism, occurring with left frontal neocortical lesion (see also cases of Stockert, 1974; Rubens, 1975).

Comment

We can discern a pattern in the different manifestations of akinesis and mutism at various levels of involvement in the nervous system. Sublimbic lesions lead to classical akinetic mutism, while, at the limbic level, the global akinetic state may be interspersed with labile affective episodes. This coincides with the differentiation of mutism out of akinesia. This dissociated facio—vocal motility then proceeds to the more selective forms of speech loss at higher levels. In accordance with this sequence, the pathological correlation proceeds from bilateral through partly asymmetric to fully asymmetric forms.

AGRAMMATISM

Agrammatism is an anterior disorder comparable to anomia of the posterior series. The condition is characterized by the relatively good use of nouns or substantives and an impairment of the small function or grammatical words. This is especially prominent in conversational speech, but it is generally present in repetition, reading aloud, and writing as well. The disturbance may be present from the start, as in the so-called one-word or holophrastic sentence: for example, the patient saying *water* or *glass water* instead of "May I have a glass of water?" This may improve to more typical agrammatic speech, as in the following example from Goodglass (1968):

> "My uh mother died uh, me uh, fifteen uh, oh I guess six months my mother pass away . . . my brother in uh Baltimore an stay all night an 'en I lef' for Florida, Mammi Beach, an uh, an uh, anen uh, Mammi Beach an stay all night and back again. Hitch hike."

With continued improvement, this leads to a stage of relatively good speech with loss of inflections, restriction of verbs to the infinitive or present tense, and an absence of unstressed grammatical words. Agrammatism has been approached as a kind of speech economy, an articulatory defect primarily affecting grammatical words, and as a true grammatical deficit.

Agrammatism is the commonest form of aphasia in dextrals with right hemispheric lesions, and it may be more common in aphasic left-handers regardless of side of lesion (Brown and Wilson, 1973; Brown and Hecaen, 1976). Agrammatism has also been described in catatonic schizophrenia, though it is by no means common in this disorder. The pathological localization is a partial or peripheral lesion of Broca's area.

In adult aphasics, there are clear relationships between agrammatism, Broca's aphasia, and transcortical motor aphasia. Agrammatism is intermediate between these forms, just as anomic aphasia, in the posterior series, is intermediate between verbal and phonemic paraphasia. In fact, the order of word "loss" in agrammatism is the opposite of that in anomia: grammatical words, verbs, and then nouns in the former; nouns, verbs, and then grammatical words in the latter. This reciprocity points to the differing contributions of the posterior and anterior systems to the final utterance at a common structural—pathological level.

ANARTHRIC (BROCA'S) APHASIA

In this disorder, the picture is that of reduced, nonfluent speech characterized by phonemic—articulatory errors. With abolition of speech, stereotypy and automatism appear. Comprehension may be well-preserved; naming and repetition may be slightly better than spontaneous speech. With improvement, there is often passage to a state of agrammatism. Writing is impaired to the same extent as speech. In those cases in which writing is markedly superior to speech, a diagnosis of "pure" motor aphasia may be considered, although the existence of this form is held in some doubt.

Patients with anarthric aphasia tend to be apathetic and passive in their behavior; there is a "loss of will" which is more common than the frustration or despair often identified with this disorder. At times, apathy gives way to euphoria or labile crying during stereotypic utterances. Awareness of the difficulty may change from moment to moment in relation to the dominant speech form, that is, volitional or automatic speech.

Although there has been much controversy over the exact borders of Broca's area, there is general agreement on the importance of the posterior part of the inferior or third frontal convolution (F3) as the site of pathology (see Brown, 1976).

Comment

A progression occurs from the partial mutism of transcortical motor aphasia through agrammatism to anarthric aphasia. In transcortical motor aphasia, there is reduced spontaneous speech, although repetition is still possible. This gives the impression of an intact production mechanism. Agrammatism represents a disruption closer to an endstage; articulations corresponding to the final grammatization are selectively involved. In anarthric (Broca's) aphasia, the defect is still closer to the final speech product, and all performances are involved. The reduced speech initiative that is observed in transcortical motor aphasia also points to an affective component. This gives way to a more active character in agrammatism. Finally, in anarthria, there is a specificity for volitional utterance and dissociation from automatic expression. As the speech act moves closer to the final utterance, the volitional and the automatic, which point to different stages, not to different mechanisms, move further apart.

The anatomical organization that supports the speech-related part of the action microgeny can be traced from systems of the sensori–motor stage through limbic structures to emerging paralimbic regions that are transitional to neocortex. Broca's area is the next level of differentiation. The lower pre-central region, the so-called face area, is not simply an effector zone for the more finely developed frontal speech cortex, but rather, at least in man, a still more recently evolved zone supporting the final phase of speech elaboration.

We see that speech, from the point of view of action, develops through a complex series of levels *parallel* to a posteriorly emerging linguistic series. The action form of speech represents an emergent that develops in a stage-by-stage *simultaneity* with the perceptual–linguistic component. The final endpoints of these two developmental series are not, so to speak, effected on some still more distant substrate; their attainment *is* the language act, the utterance.

ECHOLALIA

The problem of echolalia is central to any typology of language disorders. This is because echo responses have been observed in such a wide variety of cases, with or without aphasia or dementia, in diffuse and focal brain damage, psychosis, and as a normal stage of language acquisition.

Echolalia is not normal repetition; rather, it is a brief, precise, and often explosive response, entirely different from the approximations of child-hood imitation and quite difficult for adults to simulate. Echolalia is not entirely a reflex function since there is often "personalization" of the reiterated content, for example, the patient may repeat "How are you?" as *"How am I?"* The echo response generally has a social character and occurs only when the patient is addressed. There is also a completion effect. Thus, patients will finish incomplete rhymes or partial phrases, such as "Ham and . . . [eggs] ." The patient may correct in the echo the gram-matical form of an incorrect presentation. The disorder tends to be most prominent with the least well-understood material. This feature is impor-tant in the distinction between echolalia and voluntary repetition in which there is facilitation by familiar items. The perseverative quality of echolalia and the presence, in some patients, of an attentional disturbance has also been emphasized.

In organic cases, sporadic echo responses occur in various aphasic forms. In the so-called isolation syndrome, echolalia may be the only speech residual. Echolalia also appears as an endpoint in many progressive dementias. In cases with focal or diffuse pathological lesions, there is invariably a partial involvement of the anterior and posterior speech zones (Brown, 1975). The resultant symmetrical regression of the two speech areas explains the similarity of echolalia in dements and "isolation" type aphasics to that occurring as a final stage in speech acquisition in retar-dates.

Whether echolalia occurs as the sole form of speech or as a minor component of another disorder, there is generally a lack of awareness of the echoed content. In some cases, the echo response is accentuated as speech comprehension is lost. In both organic and functional patients, echoing without awareness may coexist with normal or pathological repeti-tion with awareness. The common facilitation of echoing with foreign or nonsense words and the occasional blocking by familiar words, the phe-nomenon of echolalia in recently acquired languages and paraphasic repeti-tion of the mother tongue, and the deterioration of repetition—from echoic to paraphasic—as a severe comprehension impairment resolves are all observations that are consistent with the view that echolalia, like the stereotypy or residual utterance, does not emerge through the full process of speech formulation. Specifically, early stages in language formulation do not contribute to the final echoic performance. There is evidence that speech or behavior that passes through a limited range of cognitive microgenesis, whether echo responses, jargon, stereotypy, or "disconnection" responses, is not accompanied by a full awareness of the content. Furthermore, the more limited range of microgenetic participation accounts for the rapid and often explosive nature of such performances.

CEREBRAL DOMINANCE

Cerebral dominance for language refers to the *degree* of left hemispheric lateralization in a given individual. Lateralization, however, is a result of specialization within the language zone of the dominant hemisphere. Thus, in the larger sense, dominance is an aspect of intrahemispheric organization. For this reason, the degree of lateralization will determine not only whether or not a patient will be aphasic after a focal lesion, but also what type of aphasia will occur.

In early life, a state of incomplete lateralization exists. Concepts of equipotentiality, plasticity, "critical period," adaptation and restitution, in so far as they concern language, have, as a central feature, the fact that lateralization is not firmly established. The duration of the process of lateralization is not known. Anatomical findings of hemispheric asymmetry in the newborn and evidence suggesting the presence of an early physiological bias of language to the left hemisphere indicate only that left hemispheric language lateralization is likely to occur, but these studies present inconclusive evidence as to the age at which this process is completed. Dichotic listening studies also suggest that dominance is established early, at least by the sixth year, but the technique cannot measure *continuing* lateralization beyond a strong right ear preference.

There is evidence to suggest that the lateralization process may continue into later life (Brown and Jaffe, 1975). This may help to account for the age specificity of certain forms of aphasia. Thus, a lesion in left Wernicke's area (namely, posterior-superior temporal convolution—T1) will produce a different form of aphasia depending on the age of the

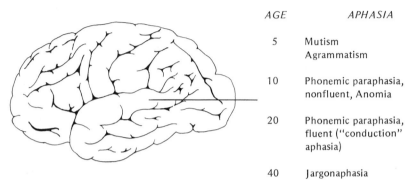

AGE	APHASIA
5	Mutism Agrammatism
10	Phonemic paraphasia, nonfluent, Anomia
20	Phonemic paraphasia, fluent ("conduction" aphasia)
40	Jargonaphasia

FIGURE 4. A lesion of Wernicke's area produces a different pattern of expressive speech at different ages.

patient (see Figure 4): in a 5-year old, a "motor" type of aphasia with mutism or agrammatism; in a 10-year old, nonfluent phonemic paraphasia or anomia; at age 20, fluent phonemic paraphasia; and, at age 40, a jargon aphasia. This age specificity is important as a rough index of degree of lateralization, while degree of lateralization is, in turn, only a manifestation of degree of intrahemispheric specification. This becomes more apparent if we consider instances of delayed or "aberrant" lateralization, as in left-handers with aphasia after lesion of either hemisphere, or in rare cases of dextrals with aphasia (crossed aphasia) after right hemispheric lesion.

Early *childhood aphasia* is characterized by mutism and/or agrammatism. Nonfluent phonemic paraphasia and word-finding difficulty tend to occur in older children. Phonemic paraphasia appears in the context of a nonfluent state, so that the picture of fluent phonemic paraphasia (phonemic or "conduction" aphasia) is rarely encountered. Verbal paraphasia is rare, while logorrhea and jargon do not occur. In fact, the latter are uncommon even in adults prior to age 30, a fact noted by Foix (1928), Isserlin (1936), and other authors.

At an early age, say less than 2 years, there appears to be a relatively even chance of developing an aphasia with damage to either hemisphere. According to Basser (1962), there is no clear lateralization prior to 14 months of age. By age 5, however, the incidence of aphasia with left-sided lesion approaches that of the adult population, although there is still a higher incidence in children of crossed aphasia. With regard to intrahemispheric localization, mutism and agrammatism can occur with damage to frontal, temporal, or parietal lobe.

Crossed aphasia refers to the combination of right hemiparesis (left hemispheric lesion) with aphasia in a left-hander, or left hemiparesis and aphasia in a dextral. In left-handed individuals, crossed aphasia occurs at a considerably greater incidence than that for aphasia with lesion of the right hemisphere. In dextrals, however, crossed aphasia is rare (Brown and Wilson, 1973).

The clinical findings in such cases are those of agrammatism and mutism, with phonemic paraphasia and anomia less common. Verbal paraphasia is rare. Patients are generally nonfluent; no instances of logorrhea or jargon have been described. The picture is similar to that of early childhood aphasia. Moreover, there is also a suggestion of more diffuse intrahemispheric language organization. At least one case of agrammatism has been described with a posterior lesion (Ettlinger *et al.*, 1955). The possibility of bilateral language representation is suggested by the deterioration of one patient after carotid injection of amobarbitol on the left side (Angelergues *et al.*, 1962). There is a "negative" case described by Boller (1973): a nonaphasic dextral found at necropsy to have an old infarct in Wernicke's area on the left side. However, the small size of this lesion leaves open the possibility of left hemispheric language, particularly if language organization is more generalized than in standard dextrals. Evidence for this was found in a personal case, a dextral adult with surgical removal of a left temporal tumor including Wernicke's area, with no pre- or postoperative aphasia, who developed an aphasia during intracarotid amobarbitol injection of the left side. This indicates that, in such patients, language is not only bilaterally organized but more diffusely organized within each hemisphere as well. The dextral with crossed aphasia may be said to have a lateralization state similar to that of a young child.

From numerous investigations, we now know that language organization is different in left- and right-handed subjects, although the nature of this difference has not yet been defined. About 75% of *left-handed aphasics* will have a left hemispheric lesion; the remainder will have a lesion of right hemisphere.

The tendency for "bilaterality" may be greater in familial than non-familial left-handers (Hecaen and Sauguet, 1971). Conrad (1949) suggested a more diffuse representation of language mechanisms in each hemisphere, and he argued that dominance in left-handers is immature relative to that of dextrals.

There are few investigations of the qualitative aspects of aphasia in left-handers. In a personal study (Brown and Hecaen, 1976), the most common feature was phonemic paraphasia or articulatory defects in the context of a nonfluent or borderline fluent state. There was commonly a reduction on a test of verbal fluency, (in which patients were required to list words beginning with a certain letter) that appeared to be strongly associated with left anterior lesion. Word-finding difficulty was common, but only a few patients showed verbal paraphasia. In such cases, verbal substitutions tended to be categorical rather than asemantic. No instances of logorrhea, semantic, or neologistic jargon were observed.

These characteristics of aphasia in left-handers are similar to those of older children and adolescents, at an age beyond that at which mutism is the most common symptom of a speech-zone lesion. Moreover, the reduced verbal fluency may represent a type of attenuated or mitigated mutism. Defective initiation may play a role in this disorder and, if so, might also explain the absence of logorrhea and perhaps the infrequency of *fluent* phonemic paraphasia.

These findings suggest that aphasia type—whether in childhood, "anomalous" dextrals, or left-handers—does not so much reflect the factor of handedness or age per se as the intrusion of a brain lesion in the course of a continual process of "leftward lateralization" (i.e., left intrahemispheric specification) which is occurring at different rates and at different levels of language learning in all three groups. In other words, there is a series of *dominance states* leading from the "anomalous" dextral → sinistral (familial → nonfamilial) → standard dextral, which corresponds to (is recapitulated by) an identical series of dominance states encountered, from childhood to adulthood, in the normal ontogenetic sequence (see Figure 5). Moreover, this progression leads from initial bilaterality and intrahemi-

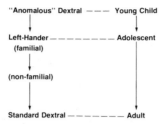

FIGURE 5. The degree of left language lateralization in ontogenesis corresponds with that in patients with atypical dominance patterns.

spheric diffuseness of representation to an increasingly more differentiated language organization within left hemisphere. Finally, there is a correspondence between the sequence of aphasic disorders which characterize stages in ontogeny—mutism → agrammatism → phonemic paraphasia and anomia → verbal paraphasia—and levels in normal language production demonstrated in adult aphasics.

LANGUAGE AND STRUCTURE

Aphasic syndromes are stages in normal language production. From the pathological material, we can distinguish two series of formative stages—a posterior perceptual linguistic and an anterior action speech—which precipitate simultaneously into the *language act*.

In the posterior series, the earliest level is that of a semantic operation, where the developing content is first shaped in the direction of representation. The word develops as an object out of somatic intrapersonal space toward an "extrapersonal" referent. Meaning is bound up with stages in this transition from self to world, a transition which is accomplished by a progression through several fields or layers. In this progression, we can trace a path from fields of wide psychological "distance," through "associative" to categorical relationships, and finally to correct word selection. The selected word—an abstract representation of that word—must then strive toward phonemic realization. This striving is more than just fitting a phonemic program to a word frame; it is a transformation to a further stage of cognition. Moreover, this entire developmental series is accompanied by a lawful unfolding—a parallel development—of other components in cognition, affect, awareness, and perception.

Similarly, the anterior series proceeds from a semantic level in action formation, where the global action incorporates the somatic space field. There is a transition from an action about the body to one that is directed outward to the forming object. Speech development appears in the emergence of facio–vocal motility within the more generalized action microgeny. This proceeds in a stepwise fashion toward increasingly more discrete constituents and ultimately to speech articulations. This is more than just a progressive differentiation; the action of speech must also move out into the world of forming objects. As with the posterior series, the anterior development is also accompanied by the parallel unfolding of an inwardly related series of other components in cognition.

This general picture of language formation is supported by a closer examination of the microtemporal relationships within and between different genetic levels.

An anatomical structure supports, and is in large measure created by, this formative process. This fact has been demonstrated by an account of the ontogenetic development of the language zones. We have seen that the bilaterality of deeper structural levels leads progressively to more asymmetrical systems. Through lateralization (intrahemispheric specification), cognition achieves a stage beyond that guaranteed by generalized neocortex. Lateralization thus appears as a continuation of the encephalization process. There is a coming to the fore, an emergence as in a figure: ground relationship, of the anterior and posterior language zones out of the more preliminary (older) limbic and generalized neocortical background. The posterior and anterior aphasic syndromes point to involvement at stages in this "vertically" organized genetic structure.

Dominance refers to the capacity of a hemisphere to carry a cognitive content to a level beyond that attainable through structural systems of the other hemisphere. In this respect, the "functions" of the two hemispheres are in the nature of successive levels in cognition rather than complementary or parallel processes. The achievement level of minor hemisphere is not isolated from that of the left side, but it is only a part of a *unitary* bihemispheric stage which, in left hemisphere, is "submerged" by the development to a still higher level.

The development of structure in relation to language and speech proceeds, in both posterior and anterior regions, from bilateral limbic, through partly asymmetric, to fully asymmetric neocortical systems. The result is the gradual emergence of two hierarchic conical fields by means of which the microgenetic elaboration of language and speech is simultaneously enacted. This simultaneity is required at each structural level and is achieved, presumably, by long "association" pathways. These pathways thus serve to modulate and so unify parallel cognitive developments and do not convey mental contents from one point to another.

LANGUAGE IN THE WORLD

We learn that in its development, language must continuously repeat its past. This past consists of stages that were, at one time, achievements in the life of the organism. Now these stages are spheres closed off from the world of the final utterance. Language also develops as a part of existing cognitive structures. It employs these structures and carries them one stage further. Language does not enlarge the world through our ability to describe it. Rather, language is one expression of an extension of cognition *into* the world. The object for which language provides a name and a concept is not there waiting to be named. In a very real sense, cognition creates the world that language seeks to describe.

The first step in the building up of the world takes place through an assimilation of the physical "out there" into an abstract somatic sensori–motor model. Language issues out of this model in the context of an action–perception development. At the same time, the language content is accompanied by other components of cognition that are also striving toward a higher form. Gradually the content breaks through to a stage at which the word exists as an object in the world. This is, in fact, the meaning of concrete language. Beyond this stage, the realization of the final utterance corresponds to a finer articulation of all other components in cognition—and, consequently, of the world—as well.

4

Action

In the preceding chapter, the proposed model of cognition was explored through a study of different forms of language pathology. In some respects, it is appropriate to begin in this way, since an understanding of the organization of more complex functions may be helpful in the study of organizational principles at "lower" stages. This is particularly true of language in relation to action and perception since language employs the same structural systems as these components but extends them to a new level. Language formation can be followed to a stage beyond that achieved (before there was language) by action and perception, while the latter can be traced back to a level out of which language first emerged.

Early in cognition, sensori–motor behavior comes to be organized into a spatial model. At this stage, perception first appears as an abstract continuation of the sensory (physical) stimulus. Similarly, action develops out of a foundation of pure motility. If movement can be taken to refer to behavior in physical space—motility outside of cognition—then *action* occurs when movement undergoes a cognitive transformation.

Initially, this first sensori—motor nucleus—the spatial model—incorporates a global axial or body-on-body motor pattern. The action is not well-differentiated; it has rhythmic or cyclic properties. At this stage, the body serves as the global referent of the action. The affective accompaniment of the action is a drive or instinct; the perceptual accompaniment is a diffuse intrapersonal pre-object. Further development of the action will carry it through a more or less symmetrical phase involving the appendicular musculature within the immediate peri-somatic space field out into the object world. The individuation of the object in "extrapersonal" space coincides with asymmetric limb action effected in a space apprehended as extrapersonal. Actually, the action together with its space is proceeding out into, and so helping to form, the extrapersonal object world. Ultimately, the action is exteriorized on the simultaneously exteriorizing object.

The temporality of this unfolding action plan derives partly from the passage from a potentiality for total simultaneous expression to completion of the total action in partial acts over time. The continual striving of the action to discharge or fill out this global precursor gives action a directional pressure. This is analogous to a directional pressure in evolution and, as in evolution, gives the appearance of purposiveness; the action seems to be striving toward an object. The action and the object, however, appear together; the object is as much the product of cognition as the act. We cannot say that an action is *on* an object or that it is directed *toward* an object, as if the desired object were there simply waiting to be moved. The final act is achieved together with the final object with only the appearance of a distance between them. This "distance" between act and object leads, through language development, to the impression of a decision-like operation. This, however, is a deception that is part of the experience of volition, but volition is much more complicated than this and is closely bound up with meaning, consciousness of, and the belief in externality (see Chapter 8).

Although the action seems to strive toward the highest attainable endstage, behavior does not simply reflect this terminal stage but is a composite of all the stages at which some condensation or discharge (i.e., lack of further transformation) of the developing action has taken place. Thus, gesture, gait, body motion, facial mimic, even tics are manifestations of the forming action at earlier levels. These appear as intermediary depositions and play their part in determining the simultaneity of multiple layers in behavior. These earlier levels provide the context, the background, within which the act is elaborated. The total act, therefore, is represented not by a single utterance or a specific performance but by the entire microgenetic structure that is traversed in its elaboration.

The action not only develops in a level-by-level correspondence with the object, but it is also formed out of the same ground as thought and affect. The thought does not stand behind the action as a kind of action plan, nor is the action influenced by the affective state. The action develops with and helps to elaborate thought and affect and is not controlled from without as an otherwise isolated set of movements. The inner relationships between these several components can be studied through an examination of pathological cases. In what follows, an attempt is made to align the various disorders of action to stages in the destructuration of the normal microgenetic sequence. In this sequence, the autonomic or vegetative stands at the threshold of the action development. From here, as a component of cognition, the action proceeds through sensori–motor to limbic and neocortical levels. The various types of action disorder, including the apraxias, are discussed in relation to the cognitive level of disruption.

ACTION AT THE SENSORI–MOTOR LEVEL

Among the organic disorders that correspond to a disruption of the *sensori–motor* level, we should include several of the striatopallidal syndromes, various dyskinesias, as well as akinetic disorders of diencephalic origin. Yakovlev (1948) has demonstrated the intermediate nature of systems subserving these (pathological) states and has emphasized the body-on-body nature of the motor disturbance. These conditions are usually referred to as "movement disorders" without careful attention to accompanying cognitive alterations. Such alterations are undoubtedly present in instances of bilateral involvement. Thus, conditions such as Wilson's disease, striatonigral degeneration, and Huntington's chorea, which preferentially involve striatal structures, all have prominent dementia. Such patients commonly have labile and excessive emotional display, bizarre, even psychotic and paranoid behavior, with schizophrenia a common misdiagnosis. A variety of other conditions involving striatal regions also show fragments of this same cognitive change, for example, "inappropriate" affect or forced smiling. These features, as well as the chorea, athetosis, and mannerisms of these patients, closely resemble certain of the schizophrenic and drug-induced states. The dementia of Parkinsonism is also becoming an increasingly more prominent and accepted feature of the disease with recent advances in drug therapy tending to benefit the "motor" and unmask the underlying "cognitive" disturbance. This is also true of the affective change, that is, depression, which is often pronounced in this disorder.

The central point to be made about these conditions, however, is not the fact that impairments of thought or affect occur; these are admittedly often minor features of the clinical picture. Rather, such impairments indicate that the movement disorder reflects a disruption in the development of action as part of, not extrinsic to, the rest of cognition; in other words, the substrate of the disorder is not a defective instrumentality played upon by more or less intact higher structures but is a disruption at an early cognitive stage. Thus, the natural history of striatal disease—from chorea through athetosis to dystonia (Denny–Brown, 1962)—may represent the reverse of that sequence of genetic levels out of which the normal action emerged. In pallidal disorders (e.g., Parkinsonism), a similar progression occurs from distal tremor through more proximal flexor-extensor conflict and tonus to a final resolution in the postural attitude of flexion dystonia. The evolution of striatal and pallidal disease also occurs along an axis of hyper- and hypo-active forms, a phenomenon that is repeated at several ascending stages in the action microgeny.

There are also changes in the volitional aspect of the action disturbance. For example, the action has a "pseudo-voluntary" character in chorea where the patient is often uncertain as to whether or not he initiated the action. For this reason, the choreic jerk may be completed into an apparently normal gesture, such as scratching the head. This may be taken as an attempt by the patient to conceal his disability. Other patients may be unaware of or indifferent to their abnormal movements. A dissociation between automatic and volitional performance is often present in Parkinson's disease. Here there may be relative sparing of "lower level" performances, such as somnambulism or coital movements, in the face of otherwise profound akinesis. These features are of more than just anecdotal interest, they are *clues to the organization and formation of the developing volitional attitude at the disturbed level.*

Although choreoathetosis, grimacing, tics, and other dyskinesiae may occur as side-effects of neuroleptic medication, there is a definite incidence of such problems in schizophrenia. Kraepelin (1919) referred to cases of this type as *athetoide ataxie*. The similarity of organic and functional action disorders was also stressed by Schilder. In schizophrenia, ideopathic dyskinesia indicates a severe regression and is associated with a poor prognosis. Mannerisms may be accompanied by delusional ideations. These have an inner bond with the delusions of passivity to a "foreign" action and the thought alienation that may presage psychotic regression and catatonic-like withdrawal. The parakinetic catatonic may have chorea and restlessness similar to that of the Huntingtonian patient. Athetotic posturing of the fingers and wrists is also common in schizophrenic patients. Spasmodic torticollis, rigidity, tremors, and tics are also similar in both groups. Kleist (1960) considered these "psychomotor" disorders analogous to organic involvements of the brain stem and frontal lobe. Encephalitic symptoms and pathology provided a bridge between the organic and the nonorganic conditions. Ey (1950) reviewed the various neurological theories of catatonia and concluded that, the deeper the dissolution in catatonia, the closer the picture to a "true motor disorder." Fixity of facial expression, grimacing, lid retraction, forced, vacuous staring, sudden laughter, and impulsive precipitate speech and movement are seen in both catatonia and organic disease, especially in certain of the hereditary extrapyramidal disorders and spastic ataxias (a personal case is described in Brown and Coleman, 1966). Abnormal attitudes, both manneristic and the more typically "organic" postures, such as flexion dystonia, are also seen in schizophrenic cases. Catatonics may lie for hours with their heads just above the pillow calling to mind similar cases of organic rigidity. The waxy flexibility of catatonia, in which the patient assumes a sustained posture to passive movement by the examiner, is seen in organic cases, particularly in advanced dements. There may also be a parallel to cases of organic dystonia mitigated by body touch. The semivoluntary resistance to passive movement (*Gegenhalten*) seen in both organic and schizophrenic patients may also belong in this category. In rare cases, even manic hypermotility may regress to a choreiform state. Nowadays such alterations are not often observed since the more profound degrees of regression can be avoided through the use of newer medications. The symptomatology then tends to reflect the more superficial (limbic) level. The fact that such regression can occur, however, establishes the continuity of the levels discussed and helps to confirm the inner identity of organic and functional symptoms of this type (see also Goldstein, 1942).

As mentioned earlier, these disorders are characterized by varying degrees of hypo- and hyper-activity. Among the hypo-active forms, akinetic mutism appears to occupy a unique position. True akinetic mutism may be related to the bradykinesia of Parkinsonism. Segarra and Angelo (1970) have defined akinetic mutism as: "a state of unresponsiveness to the environment with extreme reluctance to perform elementary motor activities. The patient lies quietly in bed, immobile, sometimes sleepy but often open-eyed and seemingly alert . . . [with] no real awareness of the events around him." The responsible lesion is usually bilateral involvement of medial hypothalamic structures (Segarra, 1970).

One view of the disorder is that both the mutism and the akinesia represent an underlying defect, a loss of the *impulse* for speech and movement. It is not clear whether akinetic mutism points to a disorder of motility or of motivation. It has been argued along anatomical lines that the syndrome results from deafferentation or disconnection of medial and reticular thalamic structures from midline mesencephalic reticulum.

Some of the experimental literature relating to this problem has been previously summarized (Brown, 1967). Lesions in the periacqueductal region produce mutism or catatonia in cats, as do lesions in surrounding reticular formation. Stimulation in this area in freely moving animals induces facio–vocal display. Unilateral lesions in man may also produce hyper- or hypo-active mimetic expression. The extent to which the cataplectic element of the narcoleptic syndrome may relate to this same anatomic zone is uncertain. In some families (Gelardi and Brown, 1957), sleep paralysis and cataplexy may be a kind of momentary akinetic mute state. The fact that laughter is a common precipitant of cataplexy also helps to relate this condition to structures of the same level underlying emotional display.

Although we do not yet have a clear picture of the nature and genesis of akinetic mutism, there may well be an important affective component. At this level, affect takes the form of instinct or drive. The interpretation of akinetic mutism as an "impulse" disorder points to a possible relationship to drive mechanisms and helps to link akinetic mutism to states such as catatonic stupor in which a primary affect regression appears more likely than a true motility disorder.

ACTION AT THE LIMBIC LEVEL

At the *limbic-presentational* level, the action is elaborated through the distal limb musculature into an extrasomatic, but still subjectively intrapsychic, space field. The action has moved out further into the world but has not yet exteriorized. In this respect, the development of the action is comparable to that of the perception, which has achieved only an hallucinatory clarity. Like the hallucination, the action is distinguished by a prominent affective element and a shift in the nature of the forming volitional attitude. The action is intermediate between the *nonpurposive* extrapyramidal stage and the *purposeful* cortical stage.

The polarity between hypo- and hyper-active forms is even more pronounced through the heightened affectivity. However, the action is not secondary to, but an inner part of, the affective state. At the limbic level, akinetic mutism proceeds to partial (more differentiated) expressions, to the selective mutism of cingulate gyrus lesions and the so-called "gait apraxia." The latter appears to represent a limbic derivative with respect to the limb musculature; it is not a true apraxia, but rather a type of akinesis at a higher level, and may well relate to involvement of fibers of the cingulate gyrus. With regard to the gait disorder, the inertia and lack of initiative may be overcome, to some extent, by certain maneuvers, such as asking the patient to dance with music. This dissociation suggests a continuity with lower (e.g., Parkinsonism) and higher (e.g., apraxic) disorders where a voluntary–automatic dissociation is also seen.

Just as the hypoactive series seems to reflect an impulse disorder, the hyperactive disorders are usually considered in relation to the predominant affective element, for example, fear and panic, aggression and (though rarely in man) rage, hypersexuality, and so on. Such conditions are seen with unilateral limbic system lesions of a convulsive type, or during depth stimulation of limbic structures in either hemisphere. It is probable that destructive or tumorous lesions of one temporal lobe also produce this effect through an irritative mechanism since such symptoms are not characteristic of stable damage or loss of one temporal lobe. Another common symptom of temporal lobe seizure is stereotyped or compulsive behavior pattern. Such phenomena are not random or meaningless. They indicate that the action is intermediate between the nonpurposive behavior of the previous level and the directed, purposeful behavior of the next level. The so-called ictal speech automatisms also belong to this category. These can perhaps be understood through a relation to dream-state phenomena and sleep speech, which also refer to the same level.

With regard to functional disorders, the cyclical motility psychosis of Kleist and Leonhard (1961) may be considered as a representation of a disruption at this stage. This condition differs from manic depression in that the affectivity disturbance is not in the foreground. The motility psychosis can be distinguished from catatonia in that the hyper- and hypoactive components do not coexist, but rather alternate. In manic-depressive psychosis, there is either reduced motility with depressed feelings and thoughts, or there is increased motility with elation in mood and thought content. The passive hypoactive state is in marked contrast to the exaggerated expressions and gestures that occur in the maniacal phase. The separate classification of catatonia, manic depression, and the motility psychosis reflects the varying accent in these syndromes of affectivity.

These conditions also have a different prognosis. There appears, however, to be an inner relationship between these forms. Thus, the occurrence in catatonia of an action bipolarity (i.e., catatonic stupor and excitation) without a strong affect nucleus leads to the affect-neutral motility psychosis in which there is alternation of the bipolar activity state. This disorder is linked to manic depression, in which the change in affect is in the foreground and also closely related to a prominent polarity in action. Each of these disorders has manifestations at several genetic planes, and within one plane there may be overlapping. For example, catatonia may undergo an expansion to mania, while manic depression may gravitate toward catatonia. The bipolar psychoses also tend toward a predominance of hypoactivity. Depression is more common than mania, and catatonic inactivity is more common than catatonic excitement. This is also true of the organic disorders. For example, in cingulate gyrus akinesia, the hypoactive state is interrupted only occasionally by "motor" outbursts.

It is at this level that impairments of an "apraxic" type first appear, namely, in the form known as ideational apraxia. This category, however, includes deficits that refer to involvements at different structural infrastages. The form of ideational apraxia specific to this stage may be termed semantic apraxia or parapraxia; the principal feature of this is a substitution of whole action sequences or partial actions during a complex performance. For example, patients will use a toothbrush to brush their shoes or will clean their nails with a screwdriver. The disorder often occurs in association with, and may be hard to distinguish from, a visual agnosia. This is not a proximity effect but points to a relationship between object and action formation. The disorder is worse for actions *with* objects than for actions in response to verbal command, a reversal of the classical hierarchy of impairment. This reflects the close bond between the preobject and actions within a limited space field. In many patients, defects in the evocation of an action suggest a similarity to anomic aphasia. This indicates a transitional relation to the next (cortical-representational) stage. This is also true of the difficulty that is occasionally seen in bimanual action, or action across the projected body midline, the spatial dislocations of the action, the tendency to utilize objects in the wrong plane or direction, or their manipulation about an incorrect axis; these all point to the neighboring stage of spatial impairment. The dementia that is often present is also in this category (see Chapt. 6).

Catatonic patients may have similar symptoms. As with ideational apraxia, there is an action disorder with what seems to be an intact effector system. As ideational apraxia is often attributed to a cognitive defect, so catatonia is conceived of as a disorder of conation without a true motor disturbance. Actually, both disorders reflect a disturbed action development, but at deep level. The catatonic patient may describe an inability to will an action, an uncertainty, an inertia, or incapacity to initiate action. The organic patient may also complain that he does not know how to proceed. In schizophrenia, substitution of one action for another (analogous) action occurs. Arieti (1975) described a patient who threw a stone instead of dropping a shoe or moved a piece of wood instead of a chair. Here the conceptual derailment is quite clear. Other patients, like ideational apraxics, will stop midway through an action sequence, forget the action, or not know how to proceed. A patient may hold a match until it burns his fingers instead of lighting a cigarette. This is not just catatonic inertia. Similar cases are described by Bleuler (1950). There may be an alternation of conflicting "innervations." This is commonly seen in organic cases. The *usual* bilateral pathology associated with the organic ideational apraxia indicates its earlier position in the apraxic series.

At the limbic-presentational level, the developing action has moved from body-on-body motility to an outward direction on the forming object. The various disorders of this transitional phase are distinguished by their prominent affective component and semantic disturbance. The transition from akinesia to semantic parapraxia, or from catatonic stupor to parapraxis in schizophrenic patients, represents a *continuum* elaborated over progressively more recent anatomical structures. We can trace this sequence in the pathological forms.

Moreover, it is conceivable that, like language and speech, action development also proceeds to a simultaneous anterior and posterior realization. The posterior sequence might, for example, occur from semantic parapraxia through an anomic form of apraxia (e.g., Marcuse, 1904; Brown, 1972) to the unit parapraxia of supramarginal gyrus lesions, the anterior series from cingulate gyrus akinesia into the various forms of oral, facial, and limb apraxia (actually, dyspraxia, as these are more closely related to *anarthric* aphasia) associated with frontal lesions. The description of individual forms of apraxia, however, has far to go before a typology such as that for aphasia can be advanced.

In the progression of forms within ideational apraxia, the beginning of the cortical-representational stage is signalled by the specific spatial disorders, the appearance of evocative difficulties in the apraxias, the more substantial control of meaning, and the trend toward asymmetry of the pathological lesion.

ACTION AT THE NEOCORTICAL LEVEL

At the *cortical-representational* level, the action has become progressively more individuated and is focused on the distal extremities. The action is directed away from the body and proceeds to a finer differentiation within the hand, then to hand preference, and finally to true handedness. Corresponding to this finer differentiation, the action achieves a full exteriorization into a space that extends beyond the body and is apprehended as extrapersonal. In achieving this autonomy in space, the action has also moved away from the object. This creates a kind of distance between the action and the object that opens up the possibility of a directional or purposive element in behavior. The action can now strive after the object, just as the object can present itself as a goal for the action. This is not a true striving, however, but a deception elaborated at this level through the continuous re-creation of action and object in a common space that is progressively more and more extended.

Among the apraxic disorders that point to this level, we must include constructional apraxia and/or so-called visual—spatial agnosia. This disorder is discussed in relation to perceptual and spatial development (see Chapter 5).

The apraxic disorders of this stage comprise a series extending from the semantic displacements of the previous level to failure in the evocation of constituent actions within the unfolding action plan. Within this series, the target action becomes progressively more clarified in the deficient performance. In the spectrum of apraxia, there is a transition from substitutions, for example, cleaning the shoes with a toothbrush, to complete failure in the evocation of the action or action component. From here, there is a transition to derailments in the unfolding of a relatively well-preserved performance, and finally to clumsy (dyspraxic) errors. This series recapitulates the sequence of levels in language production.

The form of apraxia associated with a lesion in the area of the dominant supramarginal gyrus has been termed *ideomotor* apraxia, implying an interruption between an intact idea and an intact motor apparatus. Errors are similar to those seen in the left-sided limbs of subjects with section of the corpus callosum (Sperry and Gazzaniga, 1967), namely, dextrous but inappropriate actions to verbal command and also to imitation, but improvement with object use. Both of these forms of apraxia point to a common microgenetic level. Moreover, the awareness experience accompanying the callosal form does not differ from that accompanying the unilateral form, given the presence in the latter of substituted movements of this type. There appears to be a progression from this disorder (level) to that of what may be termed "unit parapraxis." This signals the ensuing asymmetric-symbolic stage and is, in the domain of action, comparable to phonemic paraphasia in the sphere of language.

ACTION AT THE LEVEL OF DOMINANT NEOCORTEX

The developing action undergoes a transformation to the *asymmetric -symbolic* stage as an accompaniment of the new level achieved by language. Speech is one, but not the sole, representative of action at this level. Action helps to create the new space within which speech develops. The action proceeds out into this new space and to an independent status in the world. The action achieves an existence in the world comparable to that of objects. The action, however, is exteriorized *with*, not into, this object world. In this way, we see that causality is also something to be achieved.

Pathological manifestations at this level include various dyspraxic conditions, facial and a type of limb apraxia, which stand midway between action substitution and true paresis.

Limb-kinetic apraxia is a unilateral disorder of distal motility occasioned by a contralateral frontal lesion. It appears in clumsy, lost, or occasionally substituted partial actions in the face of otherwise good strength. The volitional attitude that accompanies the action development has reached the point where the patient has insight into the difficulty and frustration with his performance.

Facial apraxia is a disorder of volitional facial action appearing in performances initiated in the test situation with no alteration of spontaneous facial motility. The more automatically elicited performances (i.e., those closest to true spontaneity) are better preserved, whereas actions elicited by written or spoken commands are impaired.

Both facial and limb apraxia can occur with frontal and temporoparietal lesions. In this respect, they are comparable to phonemic paraphasia, which also occurs with anterior and posterior pathology. As in the case of paraphasia, the anterior and posterior apraxic forms at this level are extremely close in their manifestations, the anterior type appearing to be more of the nature of *dys*praxia, the posterior type a *para*praxia.

The signal change over the asymmetric level is a progression from unit parapraxis to maladroit or dyspraxic performances. This progression is similar to that observed between phonemic paraphasia and anarthric aphasia. The awareness of the action has also proceeded to a further stage. The disturbance has become more selective for volitional performances, and there is increasing recognition of error with attempts at self-correction. The action leads toward a clearly discernible goal. The action has been correctly selected, and, therefore, the goal of the action is no longer in doubt. The facilitation of performance in some cases by object manipulation occurs partly through a reduction in the opportunities for unit substitution with stabilization of the hand on the object.

Comment on Apraxia

The limited analytic material does not allow for more than a general outline of the course of action formation as inferred from the apraxia series. Nonetheless, a progression can be seen from semantic displacements without clear relation to the target action through associative, then categorical substitution, to failures in evocation of partial actions, unit parapraxis (substitutions within an otherwise well-ordered action sequence), and finally maladroitness or dyspraxia. Accompanying each apraxic syndrome, that is, microgenetic level, are specific affective and linguistic components as well as a distinct awareness experience. This series of unfolding forms is realized over a structural system organized in a fashion similar to, indeed parallel to, that of language and speech.

The so-called callosal apraxias refer to performances, generally in the left arm, that point to intermediate levels in the *unitary* action microgeny. The deficient action is identical to the semantic parapraxis of dominant temporo-parietal lesion. The only different between these conditions is that, in the latter, the achieved performance level—the semantic parapraxis—represents an endstage on apraxia testing, while, in the former, the stage can be surpassed by other actions. The apraxic performance, however, as a cognitive state, is identical in both disorders.

DISCUSSION

An action is not simply a concatenation of movements linked up temporally, guided by concepts or an "action plan," and adjusted along the way by hypothetical sensory-feedback mechanisms; rather, it is a cognitive product realized over several levels with each level represented in every performance. This process of realization can be reconstructed from a study of the pathological forms.

The Microgenesis of Action

At the earliest cognitive stage, the sensori—motor level, the action is centered about the axis of the body. The action space is the body space, and, in a sense, the body is also the referential object of the action. There is little segmentalization of the action, and there is only a preliminary articulation within the somatic space field. Pathological involvement of, or functional regression to, structures mediating this phase of the action sequence results in a series of bipolar disorders of proximal and axial "nonpurposeful" motility.

At the limbic level, the developing action moves out toward the primitive (pre-) object within a limited extrapersonal space field. The object is not fully "detached" from the intrapsychic sphere, and so the action is elaborated within a restricted range. The action goes through a semantic process in which the emerging content is shaped in the direction of the final performance. The limbic or semantic phase is also the focus of an important transformation in affectivity (q.v.), and this is a prominent part of disorders at this stage. The polarity between hypoactive and hyperactive forms persists, although with greater definition of the object and increasing separation of object and action, this polarity takes on a directed character. The disorders of the preceding stage have given way to alterations in which the volitional—automatic distinction is less clear. As with perceptual and linguistic disorders at this stage, there is little or no awareness of the deficient performance.

The action passes on to the level of generalized neocortex. The construction of an independent object (and action) space is achieved. Space is now apprehended as extrapsychic, and actions as having an influence on real objects in that "extrapsychic" space. The action is increasingly more directed toward the object, from which it has, paradoxically, moved farther apart. This change gives to the polarity of the preceding level the character of a purposive element in behavior. In the course of this development, there is a "physicalization" of the action on a simultaneously "physicalizing" object. The action achieves a veridical endstage as a causal effectuation on objects "out there" in the real world. The affect that accompanies this progression is drawn out with the action into the act and into distant objects. The action component concerns chiefly the distal musculature and performances involving or directed outward upon objects. In pathological cases, there is some awareness of error as the affective element, which goes into the formation of the awareness experience, becomes increasingly more focused on the action content.

The forming action leads ultimately to the asymmetric neocortical level. There is increasing selectivity of the action toward asymmetry and handedness. The action, however, does not go out into a world that has already formed but develops—with language—into an altogether new space. The conjoint development, which carried both action and object to their separate positions in the world, proceeds to a still greater separation and to a greater delay. The action, which has been fully exteriorized into a firmly constructed extrapersonal space, now proceeds, accompanied by a parallel object development, and, through the vehicle of language, to a further articulation of intrapersonal space. This leads to action in a mental space apprehended as such. In this way, the action becomes a sort of object for awareness. The increased delay interposed between the base level and the final action, along with this "mental" constituent of the action, helps to transform the purposefulness of the preceding level to a true volitional attitude. Pathological disturbances at this stage will involve this further (language-related) asymmetric development of facial, vocal, and limb motility, with the volitional element in the foreground of the pathology.

Structural Aspects

The physiological process that is the structural frame of this action development has an inner identity with the series of psychological transformations by means of which this development has been achieved. This process has been traced over four levels, each incorporating a complete effector system. The action organization is transformed from one state to another (in Hughlings Jackson's term, re-represented) over each successive level. In this structure, lower levels are not played upon by higher levels; rather, each level is really an existence in the world. The more global and precipitate actions of lower levels do not result from a loss of descending inhibitory control but are manifestations of that lower level as an achievement when the action development does not proceed to a further microgenetic stage.

The action develops out of an initial sublimbic layer, constituents of which incorporate parts of the wider extrapyramidal system. The body-centered action pattern then leads cephalad through phyletic-transitional planes of the limbic system which mediate a transformation to segmentalization and distal effectuation. The early organization about hypo- and hyper-active motility is maintained and further elaborated through lateral (hyper-active) and medial (hypoactive) limbic-cortical derivatives. This is seen in action disorders associated with, for example, the supplementary motor region and cingulate zone. At the neocortical level, the distally centered action moves outward to objects in the world. In man, the final cognitive transformation of the action is mediated by "motor cortex." The series then consists of the following stages:

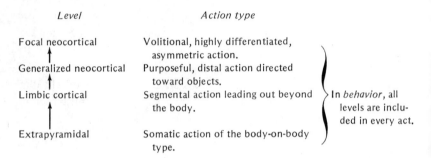

Level	Action type	
Focal neocortical ↑	Volitional, highly differentiated, asymmetric action.	
Generalized neocortical ↑	Purposeful, distal action directed toward objects.	In *behavior*, all levels are included in every act.
Limbic cortical ↑	Segmental action leading out beyond the body.	
Extrapyramidal	Somatic action of the body-on-body type.	

The so-called human "association" cortex identified with speech, facial, and limb praxis is postulated to be of less recent vintage than the precentral zone (Sanides, 1970). This corresponds to a similar relationship proposed for perceptual organization (q.v.). Evidence from the apraxias suggests that the action development may occur over both anterior and posterior structures. This seems not at all unlikely in view of the fact that language, which has this two-fold character, differentiates partly *within* the action system as opposed to having that system become secondarily associated with an acquired language capacity.

Comment on Psychoanalytic Formulations

In psychoanalytic writings, action disorders are generally viewed as the result of a decathexis or hypercathexis, a withdrawal or infusion of drive energy, upon an otherwise intact or unaltered action pattern. The action itself serves as a safety valve or discharge pathway for disturbing affect. The action is a neutral commodity played upon by cathectic forces. This assumption of an independence of affect and action is, however, too sharply drawn. While pathology suggests the possibility of a primary action regression, such as in catatonia, and a primary affectivity regression, such as in manic depression, these disorders represent only the focus of the cognitive destructuring, not the disruption of separate psychic quantities.

In this connection, the concept of drive discharge through action also seems incorrect. Both action and drive are part of a molar unit that refers to one microgenic stage. Drive energy is no more exhausted through action than action is made manifest through drive. In fact, the view that cognitive development *requires* a delay or diversion of drive discharge from the external object to the body (Rapaport, 1950) reverses the phyletic and microgenetic sequence. Central to these matters, however, is the concept of free and bound energy, which is discussed more fully in Chapter 7.

Action and Behavior

Behavior is the total action as it unfolds over time. It is impossible to adequately describe behavior. Every performance requires an isolation of some part action in a time span that is also arbitrarily segmentalized. Thus, an utterance emerges out of a ground of oral and facial motility, accompanied by gesture and affective display, and embedded in some postural set. Not only does each constituent point to a different level or phase in the formative process, but the various cognitive components clustered about each part action add to the complexity of the total behavior. One might say that each constituent action has, according to its level, a different existence in the world.

Not only is the total action distributed over the full range of microgenesis, but similar actions may have different discharge levels. Thus, one can write or play the piano automatically as well as volitionally. Yet in these similar performances, there is, however subtle, a difference in form, in awareness, in affect, in recall, and so on. This is just as true for actions that are not learned or skilled, *sensu stricto*, such as walking or even respiration, which can also be elevated to a volitional level. Clearly, it is not the body zone into which the action develops that determines the volitional attitude, but rather the transformation of the "innervation" of that zone to a higher level.

Temporality and Volition

An important aspect of action is its occurrence in a temporal sequence. There is a relationship between this temporality and the "distance" of the action from the base level. There is a progression of the action from a global and more or less simultaneous discharge to a discharge in part-acts over time. The part-acts must complete or fill out this global form. Temporality is achieved incrementally, at each successive level, as a more and more futile attempt to reconstruct the base level out of its increasingly more individuated constituents. The fact that acts seem to occur in some empirical time frame should not lead us to infer that mechanisms exist that subserve this temporal aspect; rather, a sequence is attained through a finer and finer partition within an existing order and is not a specific ordering imposed from without upon emerging contents.

This existing order is derived ultimately from processes that are fundamentally rhythmic or periodic. Within this order, sequentialization appears to be determined largely by a *selectional* process. The surface temporality would then be a reiteration of this selectional process and not the result of an independent system.

Temporality is also related to the idea of causality. A predictive sequence of occurrences underlies the inference of a causal effect. This is as true for "willed inaction" as it is for actions directed outward toward objects. The action does not have an effect on the object; the object does not have an effect on the action. The object change in a changing space is occurring even as it is approached by the action. *Causality is the imposition of the seriality of cognitive unfolding onto a happening that is everywhere simultaneous.* The problem of causality in willed or volitional action is a problem of the type: "I may will (cause) my arm to rise." Here the "I" is a substitute for an action or an object that is the cause of the intended event, that is, raising the arm. The "I" is, in fact, a product of cognition, as are the action and object. Once we understand the status of this "I" as a language-derived product actualizing simultaneously with—as a part of—other cognitive components, the deception of a causal link between the "I" and the action becomes clear. The idea of a causal relationship between "I" and action is volition; the parallel idea of a causal relationship between "I" and objects is telekinesis. The problem of the "I," the self, and the volitional attitude are more fully discussed in Chapter 8.

5

Perception

> *If ever the man shudders at the alienation, and the world strikes terror in his heart, he looks up and sees a picture. There he sees that the I is embedded in the world and that there is really no I at all . . . or he sees that the world is embedded in the I, and that there is really no world at all. . . . But a moment comes, and it is near, when the shuddering man looks up and sees both pictures in a flash together. And a deeper shudder seizes him.*
>
> Buber

The world does not come to us as a given, fully formed and waiting to be perceived; rather, it is an achievement that must be constructed by active processes. The world becomes objectivized by grades. In the course of this process, the object is transformed through various states, accompanied by different forms of awareness and affective bonds, toward the final exteriorized or "projected" image. This image is the goal of perception. We may say that perception strives toward the realization of models in the abstract that can be taken for external things.

All phenomena in perception are "mental." Those phenomena that have been treated as *physical* perceptions, such as photisms or after images, are, in fact, imaginal phenomena in abstract space.

We infer the existence of sensations preceding perceptions from the regularity of perceived events. We take this regularity for a correspondence to a supposedly real world of objects that stands behind its imaginal representation. Those philosophical authors who have written of both mental and physical perceptions, such as Brentano, have blurred the distinction between these categories. In a word, we can never know directly, immediately, that which is outside of our cognition. That which we experience directly, as in perception or in the imagination, is abstract cognitive form. In this sense, we can agree with Wittgenstein that one "can be as *certain* of someone else's sensations as of any fact."

In addition, the *extension* of the physical world does not provide an adequate basis for a distinction between the physical and the mental since extension is a special state of spatial relationships, not a separate category. Extension is not a mark of an external space, but rather characterizes one of several spaces (i.e., that of our waking life), which are elaborated in the course of cognitive development. Moreover, extension is a characteristic of visual–object and tactile perception, that is, of the space built up through these perceptions. The lack of extension in certain of the so-called sense qualities, such as color or heat (or pain), points to the fact that we deal with different types of perceptions and not with a difference as to their mental or physical status.

One can conceptualize perception as occurring in two phases. There is an initial *sensory* phase comprising the transmission to, and reception in, the central nervous system of a physical stimulus. This phase also incorporates an ensuing constructive process by means of which the stimulus is assimilated to, and thus helps to form, the spatial model of the sensori–motor stage. This sensory process can only be inferred, as it occurs completely outside awareness. The result is the assimilation of a uni-modal stimulus into an emerging abstract spatial organization, in company with sensory impressions of other modalities, in preparation for a development into perceptual awareness.

The second or *perceptual* phase concerns the cognitive transformation of the spatial model up through the described series of genetic levels leading to the final object. In the course of this transformation, the percept will undergo an initial development from a vague pre-object in a matrix of somatic motility to an imaginal or hallucinatory stage. The preobject of somatic space leads to an image *presentation* in a space field that is more extended, but still subjectively intrapsychic. The presentation refers to the thing—object, sound—that is presented and the cognitive layer in which it appears. It may also refer to the activity behind this thing at the moment of its occurrence.

A further development will carry the forming object to an existence independent of the self in a separate space. As we will see, the object is not simply projected or thrown out into the world but is, rather, exteriorized in degrees with the accompanying space form. This stage, that of the *representation*, refers to the achievement of a seemingly real object world. A final stage of development concerns the elaboration of language-related perceptions into a new space. These perceptions commence to articulate this new space field, much as the objects of the preceding level filled out and created the "external" space within which they reside. In this stage, that of the *symbol*, the perception exists for the sake of other objects.

Thus, sensations are not simply built up into perceptions, but rather they modify the otherwise independent course of cognition in the direction of the physical object. This sensory effect appears to be reiterated at multiple levels in the cognitive structure. In its absence, or through a predominance on the cognitive (perceptual) side of the process, perceptual formation will proceed along inner-directed lines. This can result in perceptions that have little or no contact with the outer world, namely, hallucinations or images, but the hallucination retraces in every other respect the microgenetic path of perception.

All sensory modalities are present in every perception. This does not mean that every visual perception has an olfactory or an acoustic element, but rather that the perception appears out of a more diffuse organization in which the various sensory qualities have an equal value. The lack of an acoustic element in a visual perception does not signify that the visual product was achieved independently of audition. The multisensory character of perception is imminent, even if not expressed, in every percept. It is by way of the process of perceptual development that the various sensory modalities enter into, and then differentiate out of, a common structure.

Perception has the effect of fusing the different senses, after which they re-emerge as abstract forms pointing back to the initial stimulus. This process of perceptual development appears to be identical, in a general way, for all sensations. There are differences, of course, in the type of space field that the perception builds up; thus, in the congenitally blind, space is defined largely by tactile boundaries; from pathological cases, there is some reason to believe that audition may not build up its own space but develops in concert with a primary visuo–tactile space field; there is also a phylogenetic scale of the sensory modalities, leading from a somatic to a fully extrapersonal localization. Naturally, there are other differences between the perceptions, such as the ability to "turn off" vision by closing the eyes in contrast to the relatively passive response to acoustic stimuli, which do not concern the present study.

The "storage" of a perception is not a process independent of perceptual formation. Rather, the realization level of each percept determines the nature of the "store." It is not a perception that is stored, but rather the full developmental process leading to the final object. Perceptual identification involves a relationship between this "store" and the momentary realization level. For this reason, identification, or recognition, has to be achieved anew at each stage in perceptual formation. In another sense, one can say that some degree of recognition always occurs prior to the final object. This problem is discussed more fully in Chapter 6.

An important part of this process of perceptual formation is an attitude of passivity which the perception generates. The passivity relates to both affect and perceptual awareness. The affective component concerns the apathetic and dependent quality attached to certain aspects (or pathologies) of perceptual development, as well as the anxiety associated with incomplete formation and the pleasure or relaxation that coincides with the appearance of the final object. The final stage of this passive attitude concerns the separation of the object out into "extrapsychic" space. There is, for example, a continuum between the passive attitude toward hallucination or imagery and its endstage as an exteriorized image (object) in the world. The passive nature of perception has a correspondence with an active quality in action formation that leads through an expanding control (volition) over objects out into extrapersonal space.

In most psychoanalytic formulations (Freud, 1960; **19**: 231; Rapaport, 1950), physical stimuli have direct access to perception, the latter being an Ego or conscious function. It is maintained that cathexes sent out into the system "perception-consciousness" enable the latter to receive perceptions, which are then passed on to an unconscious memory system. Hallucination is due to the revival of the resultant perceptual memory trace through the influence of an energy cathexis. There is also the concept of a regression of preconscious dream thought to a prior stage of mnesic imagery, with the hallucination developing as a substitute for an object gratification that has been denied.

As we will see, the object of perception does not come directly to our consciousness but is, like consciousness, the conclusion of a long chain of events. In the course of this process, not only does the perception change, but the world that the perception conveys also changes. The object world is experienced in different ways at different levels. This has also been demonstrated in the work on subliminal perception (Pötzl, 1960; Fisher, 1960). Hallucination is only one form of experience of this object world. The hallucination, however, is not a secondary change in a real perception. The hallucination is a stage on the way toward the object world.

STRUCTURAL MODEL OF PERCEPTION

With regard to the anatomical organization of systems underlying perceptual development, the general view, in the case of vision for example, is that of a two neuron pathway, from retina through thalamus to occipital lobe, that conveys information about the world to neocortex where recognition of the perception occurs. This view has been supported by evoked potential studies as well as single-unit neurophysiological investigations. The idea of cortical cell groups with specific responses to stimuli—"feature extractors," "shape detectors"—has suggested the presence of a constructive process—a series of levels of shape specification—at the neocortical level through which the stimulus configuration develops into the final object. These studies also lend support to speculations (e.g., Kohler, 1951) on the possibility of a psychophysical isomorphism in visual perception.

If we study the anatomy of the visual system, however, we discover that the (predominantly afferent) fibers are distributed to each of the described hierarchic levels. The initial projection to medial geniculate body is in relation to the sensori–motor level through intrathalamic conduction, and there is, of course, even in man, an important visual organization in tectum. Fibers leave the optic radiations and distribute to the limbic system (MacLean, 1972) en route to striate cortex, and there is the major projection to the striate cortex proper. In general, this pattern is the same for other perceptual systems as well. Olfaction does not have a thalamic representation, but the distribution to amygdala and pyriform cortex accomplish the assimilation of olfactory sense data to at least the first two structural levels.

This organization is consistent with the following hypothesis: the sensory signal at the earliest (sensori–motor) stage acts to shape or determine the incipient spatial model in the direction of that signal, thus turning cognition away from autonomous goals. This process will then be reiterated at each successive structural level; the effect is a repeated re-submission of the forming percept to sensory modeling at progressively higher stages. This modeling effect would not be the same at all levels but would change in a manner parallel to the developing perception. The central point, however, is that the main work of perceptual development is carried out in the cognitive structure itself, that is, over the discussed phylo-ontogenetic strata, and not in the sensory pathways. Accordingly, the visual "input" at striate cortex comes, so to speak, after the perception is almost complete. The hierarchy of "feature extractors" at the neocortical level would then build up the sensory configuration so as to add the final modeling on the perception emerging from the limbic stage. This concept is schematized as follows:

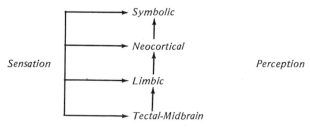

This formulation agrees with current research on the so-called double or dual visual system (Sprague, 1966; Schneider, 1969) and with evidence for at least two levels of visual perception in animals (e.g., Lashley, 1948) and man (Bender and Krieger, 1951). In human cases of cortical blindness with bilateral destruction of striate cortex, there is also evidence of persistent visual function (e.g., Brown, 1972). Trevarthen (1974) has interpreted findings in split-brain subjects in terms of an "ascending" hierarchic model of visual perception. Trevarthen's notion of diffuse (gestalt-like) and focal systems as *parallel* organizations would, in our view, correspond to *successive* levels in percept formation.

This hierarchy of levels corresponds to stages—and pathological disorders—in the microgenetic path of percept formation. It leads from a stage of subcortical perceptual change through a limbic level, characterized by hallucinatory and related phenomena, to the various cortical syndromes. In each disorder, one can recognize negative and positive effects; the former refer to the reduced level of perceptual realization, the latter to a cognitive process no longer determined by sensory modeling with an intrusion into the final perception of internally structured contents (pre-perceptions).

BRAINSTEM—TECTAL DISORDERS

Disorders of perception at the *sensori—motor* stage, that is, involving midbrain (tectum), have not been the object of thorough study. Conceivably, the condition of progressive supranuclear palsy (Steele *et al.*, 1964) characterizes disruption at this stage, the pathology sparing cortex and distributed chiefly in pallidum, upper brainstem, and cerebellum. In this condition, there is a gradual disintegration of visual—spatial ability and correlated axial motility. The progressive limitation of eye movements, which is uniformly present, does not appear to be secondary to interruption of a cable-like system controlling gaze, but rather it occurs together with a dissolution of visual space (Constantinidis *et al.*, 1970; personal cases) and points to an underlying cognitive disorganization. Performance on visuo-spatial tasks or writing in such patients is considerably worse with the eyes closed than it is in patients with peripheral blindness or in normal blindfolded subjects.

The perceptual regression seen in this disorder may not be dissimilar to that observed in some schizophrenic patients, at a final stage of catatonic vegetism. Such patients also show fixity of gaze, loss of spatial values, and disintegration of the object world. Moreover, the condition appears in the regression of an hallucinatory state, that is, as an undermining of the ground out of which the hallucination has developed.

LIMBIC DISORDERS

At the level of the *limbic presentation*, the perception takes the form of a hallucinatory experience. This may occur as an apparent distortion of or intrusion into a veridical perception, or the perception may be completely replaced by hallucinatory content. The hallucination approximates an image or a perception according to the degree of exteriorization achieved, and this, in turn, is closely linked to the amount of hallucinatory distortion and the extent to which the hallucination dominates the perceptual field.

The hallucination may be carried out to a position in external space, or cognition may be drawn back to the hallucinatory level, as occurs normally in dream. The space of the hallucination, which is outside the body, also contains the body, as in a fluid medium. This space is an almost tangible product; it is a more concrete space between that of hallucination and perception. It is said, for example, that the perceived space of the schizophrenic is lacking in depth (Weckowicz and Sommer, 1960).

There is often a progression in the character of the hallucination. We see this in both organic and functional cases. Visual hallucination may begin with photisms or vague unformed images, with metamorphoptic experiences, or even with memory images. In the case of audition, there may be tinnitus, noises, or the sound of a name. Organic hallucinations are ordinarily not as persistent as functional hallucination, and, in the former, visual hallucination is more common. These, however, are quantitative features and do not point to an inner difference. De Morsier (1938) has demonstrated that organic and functional hallucination are identical in all sensory modalities. In both organic and functional cases, persistent hallucination leads to a gradual usurpation of the microgenetic level more and more completely by the hallucinatory material. One might say that the hallucination becomes invested with the thought content that it replaces at that level. In this way, the hallucination takes on the character of psychotic thought.

There are several forms of *organic* hallucination. In the syndrome of peduncular (brainstem) hallucinosis, the pathology of which is not precisely know, there are "multimodal" hallucinations, often of faces, animals, insects, or occasionally formed scenes. In content, there is a similarity to hypnagogic imagery (vide infra). There is commonly a fused auditory component, and some patients will even describe their "verification" of the reality of the hallucination by touch. Generally, there is initial awareness of the imaginal nature of the hallucination, but, if the problem persists, a psychotic hallucinosis will develop. Some patients have been described who believe in the reality of the hallucination during the attack but recognize its imaginal basis after the attack subsides. Hecaen (1972) cites a case of Schilder's that is instructive in this regard.

The more frequent type of hallucination in organic patients involves the temporal lobe. Again the visual component tends to predominate, but there is often fusion of several perceptual systems. Formed scenes, often mnemic images, and metamorphotic distortions are most common. Horowitz and Adams (1970) have described formed hallucination with both depth and surface stimulation in the temporal lobe of waking subjects.

Another class of organic hallucination concerns the various cortical syndromes associated with a lesion in the pertinent "sensory projection" area. Thus, a lesion involving the "primary" visual cortex entails visual hallucination, such as the usual occurrence of visual hallucination after cortical blindness. Commonly the hallucination is especially prominent in the most severely involved sectors of the visual field. Similarly, a lesion of the somaesthetic cortex will entail alterations in tactile and kinesthetic perception (e.g., phantom limb phenomena or duplications); uncinate lesions result in olfactory hallucination, and so on. In the syndrome of "word deafness" with lesion affecting primary auditory cortex, auditory hallucination is a relatively constant finding, usually consisting of a few words, a sentence, or some unintelligible sounds. There is no satisfactory theory explaining this relationship between lesion of the cortical perceptual zone and hallucination confined (predominantly if not completely) to the damaged modality. Previous accounts have stressed the liberation of "memory images" stored in "association" cortex no longer under "input" control. Actually, these hallucinations represent the highest (i.e., neocortical) level achieved by a preperception deprived of the final cortical modeling.

Descriptive studies for the most part have concerned *functional* hallucination. In schizophrenia, hallucinatory states commonly begin with an initial aberration of the real object. Colors appear brighter and more intense, perceptual constancy may break down, a sound may become a whisper, a smile a sinister grimace. These apparent "sensory" changes often precede autonomous image formation. In other cases, the memory image may appear as an antecedent of psychotic hallucination. The transitional relationship between the memory image and the hallucination is seen in the evolution of the scenic hallucination of drug intoxication. The hallucination may begin with an unraveling of a perceived object; there is a loosening of object boundaries, a change in the characteristics of object space, instability of color–object relationships, distortions of shape, and so on. This initial elaboration on the real object may become a hallucination that is independent of the object surround with the characteristics of a memory image. This may proceed to semantic change in the hallucination with the appearance of highly symbolic content with a strong affective tonality. This progression from morphological distortion through mnemic imagery to semantic displacement retraces the genetic path of percept formation. It also corresponds to the sequence of levels in visual agnosia.

In early psychosis, an hallucination may appear alongside a veridical perception. The hallucination has the character of an image in consciousness that is apprehended by an exterior awareness. This is the feeling of passivity to foreign thoughts, the so-called *automatisme superieure*. Although hallucination and veridical perception may coexist, they do not inhabit the same space. During hallucination, normal perception cannot be maintained. Schizophrenic patients show a lack of auditory comprehension during bouts of auditory hallucination. This is true also of organic cases, and it is not due to distraction or "auditory inattention," since fragments of the perceptual material can appear in the hallucinated content. Similar phenomena occur in sleeptalkers who reiterate with consonantal or assonantal change the heard speech of others. The perception, therefore, does not persist unchanged alongside the hallucination in a common space field; rather, one tends to be incorporated into the other.

There may be a relationship between the "sensory" modality of the hallucination and the occurrence of psychosis. In schizophrenia, the predilection for auditory hallucination—and the consequent relation to language—may hasten the development of a lasting psychotic state. In organic cases, psychosis is more prominent with auditory than visual hallucination. In word deafness, psychosis is almost always present, at least initially. Patients are commonly hospitalized on a psychiatric service until the organic nature of the disturbance becomes clear.

NEOCORTICAL DISORDERS

The pathology of visual perception at the *cortical-representational* level begins with an object that has developed out to a position in extrapersonal space and has become "detached" from its intrapsychic origins. The object also has, to varying degrees, emerged through the previous semantic or selectional phase, and, therefore, the endstage of the perception is less doubtful. Defects in object recognition (agnosia) are characteristic of this level. (See Brown, 1972, for a full discussion of these disorders.) These include impairments with objects in a structurally similar class (e.g., faces), objects in general, and letters qua objects. The pathology of these defects is bilateral posterior parietal (or parieto-occipital) lesion.

Elements of this condition have classically been referred to as "associative" visual agnosia, emphasizing a dissociation between the poor visual—object recognition and preserved "basic" visual function, for example, object drawing and tactual identification. In a given case, recovery tends to occur in the following direction: words, objects, faces. This sequence is the reverse of that encountered in the endstage occipital lobe syndromes (i.e., "apperceptive" agnosia). Thus, the "associative" (neocortical) agnosic reads in the presence of poor object recognition, while the apperceptive (asymmetric neocortical) agnosic recovers object recognition before reading, that is, evolves to a "pure" alexic.

Patients with impaired facial recognition are termed prosopagnosic. Here the problem is clearly as much one of perception as of "perceptual identification." Patients can draw the unidentified object, but the reproduction is inaccurate, and they show, by a variety of tests, that they do *not* have normal perceptions (Brown, 1972). The fact that the defect involves a perceptual category, and the association with (bilateral) temporo-occipital pathology, helps to establish a relation to defects in semantic processing of the preceding level.

This defect may resolve out of, or progress to, a visual object agnosia. Whereas in prosopagnosia the constituents of the object, such as a specific face, cannot be discriminated although the object class is known, in "associative" agnosia, the constituents of an object *can* be identified once the object itself is recognized. Once the patient has been given the name of an otherwise unrecognized object, he can identify its component parts. Such patients commonly misidentify objects so as to suggest semantic factors. Responses such as "It isn't a cat" to a picture of a mouse, or categorical impressions, such as "fruit" for an apple, are not uncommon. The defect in perception is comparable to that of verbal paraphasia and anomia in language production. The reading difficulty in these patients is also global or semantic, for example, the patient reads *horse* as "zebra."

Schizophrenics with disruption at the preceding (limbic) level may pass into the sphere of an object agnosia. This does not refer to a loss of the "object bond"; such patients make definite agnosic errors. There is inability to recognize or comprehend the use of everyday objects, and semantic errors occur on tests of object identification. Disorders of drawing have also been described in schizophrenic patients that are similar to those seen in organic constructional disability. Moreover, schizophrenia is commonly preceded by a phase of perceptual breakdown. The so-called delusional perception becomes evident when the patient attributes unusual significance to a (presumably) normal perception. This symptom has been shown to reflect a loosening in perceptual coherence in association with a freer play of verbal association (Matussek, 1952). Here we see that the cognitive regression may have a focus either in the perceptual or in the linguistic sphere. In addition to the perceptual regression, the percept fails to attain full exteriorization. This is another way of talking about the concretization of the object. There are also descriptions of cases in which there is an inability to perceive wholes. A patient may focus on only a part of an object and proceed to smaller and smaller fragments. This phenomenon has been termed *aholism* and may have some relation to the condition of simultanagnosia in which patients are unable to attend to more than one object at a time in the visual field.

Disruption at the cortical-representational level will have a prominent effect on the developing space field. There is a transition to an extrapersonal space as space becomes articulated, actually elaborated, by objects.

ASYMMETRIC NEOCORTICAL DISORDERS

The series of neocortical disorders of perception is transitional to another group clustered about the perceptual endstage. These include "apperceptive" agnosia and agnosic (or "pure") alexia. In the former, there is bilateral occipital lobe pathology; in the latter, there is ordinarily a lesion of dominant occipital lobe and posterior corpus callosum.

In apperceptive agnosia, there is an impairment in the recognition (identification) and discrimination of visual, and occasionally tactile, stimuli in the presence of fairly good intellectual ability. Patients can often describe from memory objects that cannot be identified. Close examination of such patients reveals that the difficulty in object recognition corresponds to the structural complexity of the presented item. There is often facilitation of performance by simple uniform stimuli. On discrimination tests, performance deteriorates with disparate stimuli; such stimuli act to increase the overall complexity of the array. At times, only a line drawn before the patient or a movement in the visual field can be identified. The disorder often appears in the resolution of a cortical blindness. Such patients may be slow and apathetic. Visual imagery and visual dream may or may not be lost, but generally there is poor recollection of visual material previously seen.

With recovery, the disorder characteristically resolves to an agnosic alexia with inability to read in the presence of good writing and object recognition. Such patients read through a process of "literal analysis," in a slow, letter-by-letter manner, often guessing at the latter half of the word. There is a clear relation to the length of the word to be read, and errors commonly reflect morphological relations to the stimulus item.

These two conditions, "apperceptive" agnosia and agnosic or "pure" alexia, are not defects of the in-processing of visual information but *represent successive levels in the terminal phase of a productive perceptual process.* The pathology of each disorder is consistent with this interpretation. It is quite possible that a callosal lesion, particularly with pathology in the dominant hemisphere, acts to diminish or alter function in the minor hemisphere. If so, this would result in a mild bilateral syndrome in the agnosic alexic and a more severe bilateral syndrome in the apperceptive agnosic. In other words, the syndrome is determined by the residual functional capacity of a bioccipital field. The specificity for left-sided pathology may derive from a biased left–right effect on homologous cortex, perhaps relating to dominance establishment through callosal-mediated right hemisphere inhibition.

There is clinical evidence for this relationship. This type of alexia usually appears in the resolution of a cortical blindness or a difficulty in object recognition. The latter has been attributed to object-naming difficulty or verbal amnesia through, respectively, parietal or temporal lobe involvement. Closer study of such cases in the acute stage, however, should establish the *agnosic* nature of this impairment. Furthermore, object misidentification can be induced in the alexic through brief tachystoscopic exposure. Moreover, the type of alexia is similar in both disorders. The "apperceptive" agnosic may read some letters, but the "pure" alexic can also, and, in both disorders, visually simple letters, such as X or O, are usually preserved. In sum, agnosic or "pure" alexia is not the result of a "disconnection"; rather, it is a type of *partial* apperceptive agnosia brought about by a functional reduction in the otherwise intact right occipital lobe.

With complete bilateral lesion of striate cortex there is cortical blindness. The degree to which the pathology involves neocortex surrounding the striate zone will determine the level of the remaining preperception, that is, whether or not imaginal phenomena are present. Such patients do not behave like myopes or like normal subjects wearing blindfolds. Gait may be confident, even aggressive, without groping. There is minimal bumping into objects. This suggests a perceptual experience at an inferior level. Patients commonly deny that they are blind, a denial which the examiner should perhaps take more seriously. The hallucinatory phenomena that usually accompany this disorder, at least in the initial stages, do not reflect a liberation of a visual "store," but rather point to the level realized by preperceptual contents lacking completion to the perceptual endstage.

PERCEPTION OF ORAL LANGUAGE

The perception of oral language is not grafted onto auditory perception as a higher achievement but develops out of the earliest cognitive stages. The disorders of oral language perception begin at a semantic level, where word and object are in closer union, and proceed to defects at the final phonemic or morphemic realization of the perception in abstract auditory space.

In the posterior (fluent) aphasias, disorders of speech comprehension have some relation to the pattern of expressive speech. A change in expression from, for example, neologism to phonemic paraphasia, or from jargon to semantic paraphasia, is accompanied by a change in comprehension. This is not as clearly the case in anterior (nonfluent) aphasia in which speech loss may be accompanied by differing grades of perceptual deficit.

Evidence for an orderly series of perceptual deficits in the posterior aphasias is found in several works (Kleist, 1962; Pick, 1931; Brown, 1972). At an early stage, the disorder takes the form of semantic errors, impairments in the understanding of word meaning; words may be repeated without comprehension, and phonemic discrimination will be preserved. This can also be seen in schizophrenic patients. Intermediate forms (levels) in the pathological series center on specific comprehension impairments linked to anomia and fluent phonemic paraphasia. (In this regard, see Zurif *et al.*, 1974.)

In word deafness, there is inability to comprehend (i.e., perceive) speech sounds and, to some extent, musical sounds, although hearing is spared and serves to distinguish the disorder from cortical deafness. Luria (1966) maintains there is a defect in phonemic hearing (cf. Brown, 1976a). Word deafness, however, is not a first-order impairment of speech "reception" but a disruption at the *final* stage in the speech perceptual series. In the transition from the semantic to the phonological level, auditory perception emerges from a peri-somatic matrix into abstract extrapersonal space. Disorders of the distal segment of this process, such as word deafness, may show preservation of actions involving axial or midline body musculature in response to verbal commands. Such patients also respond to intonation and can distinguish jargon from real speech. These performances point to stages in the perception that have been completed prior to the pathological level.

PERCEPTION AND COGNITION

Microgenesis of Perception

Perception is an active, dynamic process that is directed toward the reconstruction of an object. The degree to which this process is completed determines the extent to which the object is reconstructed. The final object (or realization level) can exist in different forms and each form reflects—*is*—an external world. One can say that there are as many inferred real worlds behind the object as there are levels of object realization.

The process of perceptual formation is conceived of as a series of at least four such levels or phases corresponding to the described stages of cognition. At the initial stage, the developing cognitive form, the perception to be, is shaped or determined by sensory information in the direction of the external object. The resultant *model* is then transformed to the next (limbic) level where a reiteration of sensory control helps to maintain cognitive development in the direction of the object. Subsequently, the emerging preperception is transformed through neocortical secondary (e.g., prestriate) and primary (e.g., striate) zones.

In visual perception, this process has been traced from (*1*) a subcortical level where the global precursor of the perception (spatial model) exists in an intrapersonal somatic space field, through (*2*) a limbic level of semantic realization (distortion, displacement, condensation), where the developing object (presentation) exists in an extrapersonal but subjectively intrapsychic space, to (*3*) a neocortical level where the selected object (representation) is exteriorized into a space apprehended as extrapsychic, and finally to (*4*) an asymmetric stage where the object (symbol) takes on a new value as a part of language development. These stages are marked not only by an increasing delimitation of the object and its gradual movement outward to a position in external space, but also by a progressive change in all other components of cognition as well. Thus, disorders of object formation will be accompanied by alterations of affect, thinking, and consciousness specific to the level of impairment.

The degree to which the object is selected (emerges) will determine the nature of the final percept. This appears in pathology as an impairment of object recognition. This impairment fluctuates from one moment to the next, at one time closer to the semantic level, at another closer to the final object. This fluctuation may occur in relation to external objects, in relation to imagery, or in relation to both.

Imagery and Dream

With absent or reduced sensation, perception will proceed along autonomous lines into hallucinatory or imaginal forms. There is a continuum from the semantic distortion of dream or psychotic hallucination, through intermediate hypnagogic forms where "associative" links or simple fusions are evident, to the memory image that is "true to experience." The memory image differs from the hallucination in that it is further along in the process of percept formation. The hallucination is an incompleted memory image. This is why the memory image is more common in transitional (hypnagogic and hypnopompic) states, as midway between the hallucination and the waking perception. This transition from hallucination to the memory image is—as in the series leading to the external object—marked by a change in affect, in awareness, and in the space of the image. The unbidden, semantically distorted hallucination, which is taken as real, evolves by degrees to the partly volitional, undistorted memory image with clear awareness of its imaginal character. This sequence is often reversed in psychotic decompensation. Indeed, hallucination often begins as a memory image. In sensory deprivation, memory images occur as an initial stage. In transitional or hypnagogic states, an evolution occurs from a memory image through autosymbolic or hypnagogic imagery to complex dream hallucination. This autosymbolic image (Silberer, 1951) is, to some extent, volitional. In this respect, it is midway between the memory image and the hallucination.

The space of the image differs from that of the final object. When image and object occur together, they not only occupy a different space, but there is also a replacement of one by the other. The image fills a nonapprehended void in the perception.

A perception that is revived immediately is an eidetic image; on the other hand, after a delay, it is a memory image. During this delay, the image undergoes a change; it becomes, so to speak, invested with cognitive content. Because of this delay, the memory image is also less vivid. In contrast, the eidetic image is not a part of the life of the individual. According to Jaensch (1920), eidetic phenomena are intermediate between perception and true memory images. Busse (1920) maintained that the afterimage, the eidetic image, and the memory image represent progressively higher states in a teleological continuum. There is also a resemblance between the eidetic and memory image in relation to affective tone (Lukianowicz, 1960); these images, unlike the hallucination or the perception, do not bring forward new content.

The work that memory carries out on the perception continues well beyond its "registration." The memory image expands until its perceptual character is indistinct. Ultimately, the perception is lost altogether, and the memory image takes on the character of a thought. In the same way that the perception is "invaded" by memory, the hallucination also becomes "invested" with thought.

In dream, the memory image dissolves through transitional phenomena to the hallucination. This coincides with a coming to the fore of internally structured contents. Space, awareness, and affectivity also recede to earlier levels. The dream perception is a manifestation of limbic stage contents that are intermediate to the final object in the waking state.

On the Psychoanalytic Theory of Perception

In psychoanalytic theory, the relationship between the memory image and the hallucinatory distortion is accounted for by a censorship on emerging ideation. This results in the displacement and condensation characteristic of the dream work. The failure of a content to fully develop, however, is not a sign that it is actively prevented from doing so. The failure to find distortion in the memory image does not mean that the memory image has not gone through the same process as the hallucination. The memory image has, in fact, successfully completed that level at which the hallucinated object remains fixed. Analytic theory also proposes that the hallucination arises as a substitution for a wish fulfillment. This can also be said of perception. The wish relates to the "intrapsychic" phase (i.e., prior to exteriorization) of the perceptual process.

There is also a different affect accompaniment of the forming percept at different levels. This has been the subject of an important study in the recognition of tachystoscopic figures by Sander and Wohlfahrt (see Conrad, 1947). In such experiments, anxiety accompanies the preterminal or pre-Gestalt phase in percept formation. There may be a relation also to the so-called Zeigarnik effect in which a tension system (Lewin, 1935) is set up by incompleted tasks. We do not have to consider the hallucination and the perception as unrelated contents by virtue of their differing affective tones.

Freud raised the problem of why there is belief in the reality of hallucination and not of clear visual images and suggested that, in the former, withdrawal of cathexis from consciousness resulted in suspension of reality testing. The hallucination, however, is not invariably accepted as a real perception. This is related to the degree of semantic distortion in the hallucinated content and, therefore, to the microgenetic level of the hallucination. The closer a hallucination approaches to a memory image, the more developed is the awareness experience. The hallucination and the memory image are not objects for awareness but play a part in determining—constructing—the accompanying awareness form.

Perception and Consciousness

Perception, like action or language, is elaborated over levels, and each level contributes to the final performance: the object in perception. When a hallucination intrudes upon a perception, the normal participation of the earlier level in that perception is magnified. A persistence of the hallucination, that is, persistently incomplete perceptual development, tends to draw cognition back to the hallucinatory level. Consciousness will also regress to that of the pathological level. Ultimately, this can lead to an hallucinatory psychosis. There is a waking dream-like state in which the hallucination—the dream—represents the endpoint not only of perceptual development, but also of all cognitive development.

This concept of a perception that is formed over several stages also implies that the world is realized at levels corresponding to those of perceptual development. The final object is not a truer depiction of the real world than is an intermediate product. For the perceiver, reality is the momentary achievement level of the perception. In other words, reality depends on how far the world—the perception—can be objectified.

Each level in perception embodies, or is a part of, a distinct state of consciousness. *Within that state*, the perception is taken to be true. This is why a dream is judged to be real during the dream. Waking perception contains within it, as a precursor, the microgenetic dream state: There is a recollection, as in a memory image or a shadowy amnesic segment, of the earlier dream level. Dream, however, does not contain a knowledge of the waking level, for the latter represents a stage toward which the dream level is directed but which it has not yet achieved. In dream, we know nothing of levels that lie beyond; therefore, in waking perception also, we cannot fathom the possibility of an even higher level in relation to which the waking percept stands as a type of dream.

6

Thought and Memory

I do not recognize memory in the sense in which you mean it. Whatever we encounter that is great, beautiful, significant, need not be remembered from outside, need not be hunted up and laid hold of as it were. Rather, from the beginning, it must be woven into the fabric of our inmost self, must become one with it, create a new and better self in us and thus live and become a productive force in ourselves. There is no past that one is allowed to long for. There is only the eternally new, growing from the enlarged elements of the past; and genuine longing always must be productive, must create something new and better.

Goethe

Thought and memory are different terms for a common process. Thinking is a way of characterizing certain aspects of memory, while remembering is a way of characterizing certain forms of thought. Thought and memory are directional features of the essential components of cognition[1] —action and perception, of which language is a derivative—but

[1] Cognition refers to mind or mentation, not specifically thinking (see Preface).

are not themselves special functions. Thought and memory enter into every cognitive performance, but they enter from *within*, not as aids or determinants. Thus, a full account of any one component of cognition is an account of the nature of thought and memory.

In perception, thought refers to aspects of the content at successive levels. Dream perception, no less than waking imagery, is a form of thinking. Problems of "stimulus generalization" or of concrete and abstract thinking are bound up with stages in object formation. We speak of memory when perception is given over to reproduction, as in certain forms of imagery. Imagery, however, can also be productive, and then it is termed thought. Thought does not stand behind the components of cognition and give them direction, nor is memory a special mechanism, or set of mechanisms, to which these components have access. Rather, thinking and remembering are descriptions of modes of cognitive employment. They are ways of looking at other primary components. Apart from these components, thought and memory have no psychological or anatomical reality.

THOUGHT

At early stages in cognition, the expression of a thought is direct, global, and immediate. The expression of the thought in action or perception constitutes the content of the thought; the expression *is* the thought. We may speak of instinctual thought in relation to this early stage.

Subsequently, the content will pass through "layered" semantic fields, through a selectional process that is central to all forms of precategorical ("primitive," paleological, or paralogical) thought, as well as to creative thinking. In pathological states, this level concerns psychotic thinking, derealization, and loss of objects.

The endpoint of the semantic phase is the attainment of representational adequacy. Later stages in the achievement of representation are bound up with "spatial" and "categorical" thinking. The continued differentiation of the object out of a pre-object of more generalized features and the final exteriorization of that object in extrapersonal space are processes that elaborate the space-dependent properties of thinking. Indeed, it is probable that the ability to perceive exteriorized objects in an articulated space field *presupposes* an apprehension of relationships between those objects, that is, some degree of abstraction. To the extent that the organism can move from the general to the specific in the formation of the perceptual world, it can also move from the particular to the class. *The ability to generalize upon a specific object is not a secondary accomplishment, but rather a revival of more preliminary forms in the process of object formation.* Similarly, the substitution in conditioning techniques of one signal (i.e., a perception) for another through close temporal presentation points, not to a secondary linkage, but to the common preperceptual background of both stimuli. Pathological disorders at this level consist chiefly of the dementias. Here space organization undergoes disruption in association with defects in abstraction, that is, in object relations. There is also an encroachment on language at the same level, with word-finding difficulty or anomia.

In the final symbolic phase of thought development, cognition is elaborated through language into a new space. Language begins to articulate the frontiers of the intrapersonal space that was left behind in the outward movement of action and perception. Language invades, populates, and thus builds up this new "inner" space and, in this way, draws out or delays the expression even more. Language establishes a mental sphere that seems to be opposed to the space of objects. The further separation of "language space" from the space of objects is an important part of introspection, or consciousness of, and the volitional attitude. Introspection, however, does not generate thought. Language enlarges thinking by giving to cognition a development other than that of objects. Language adds content to the semantic fields of objects. Pathological disorders of thinking at this stage occur in relation to the described asymmetric language-related syndromes.

Pathology of Thought

Traditionally the dementias have been classified according to disease type (e.g., Pick's or Alzheimer's disease) or area of primary involvement (e.g., frontal or temporo-parietal). A distinction has also been made concerning the presence of focal deficits, age of onset, and rapidity. The various organic dementias, however, do not differ *intrinsically* from the "functional" thought disorders. There is a continuum from psychotic thought to general paresis to organic (Alzheimer's, Pick's) dementia that retraces the path of cognitive formation. This series of disorders of thinking differs from the "component" disorders (e.g., aphasia, apraxia) in that the disruption (cognitive level) is distributed over all components rather than affecting one component preferentially. Such component disorders that do occur in dementia, for example, alterations in language or perception, will always be characteristic of the specific cognitive level to which the thought disorder refers. Thus, we see word-finding difficulty in diffuse neocortical involvements, semantic language alterations in psychotic thinking, agnosic errors in Alzheimer's disease, and hallucinations in psychosis and regressed cortical dementia. These defects in language or perception point to the incorporation of those components by the level-specific regression that accounts for—*is*—the dementia or thought disorder.

PSYCHOTIC THOUGHT DISORDER

This consists of various elements that differ according to the psychotic type. Thus, "flight of ideas" is most characteristic of manic patients, while perceptual delusions are most characteristic of schizophrenia. Most of these symptoms, are revealed through the language of the patient, and, when we look closely at these language products, we see close relations to the aphasias. The symptoms of psychotic thinking incorporate language changes that point to the structural level of the cognitive impairment. The "chance linkages" of flight of ideas, the verbal and clang associations, closely recall similar features in aphasic jargon cases. The perseverations, blocking, and inhibitions in the language of psychotics are also common features in aphasic patients. Illustrative cases are described by Kinsbourne and Warrington (1963) and Kreindler *et al.* (1971).

The main feature of delusional thinking is the appearance of a new content in cognition and its acceptance as real by the patient. The delusion is linked to the obsession. The delusion appears in relation to ideas, that is, language, and to perceptions (as in delusional perceptions), while the obsession is related to ideas and to motor acts (compulsions). The fact that the obsession does not bring forth new content and that it is recognized for what it is points to a later stage in cognition; in other words, the delusion and the obsession concern different levels, not different mechanisms. This also explains why the obsession persists but is under some control, while the delusion, which is a type of semantic deviation at a deeper level, tends to draw cognition into the delusional content. This leads either to delusional psychosis and loss of reality or to systematization of the delusion within the semantic frame that is generic to the original deviation.

Most approaches to schizophrenic thinking have attempted to elicit a central deficit in terms of which the disorder can then be explained (see review in Chapman and Chapman, 1973). Examples are: loss or change in abstract attitude, excessive generalization or overinclusion, and impaired experiential "filtration." An important line of study has emphasized a defect in logical relationships (Arieti, 1975). The thought of the schizophrenic points to an inferior level in logical thinking, namely, paralogic, and is based on the principle of von Domarus (Domarus, 1944) that an identification of dissimilar subjects on the basis of a shared predicate(s) leads to aberrant products in thought and language: for example, Mary is a virgin; I am a virgin; therefore, I am the virgin Mary. Some efforts to refute this theory have employed a multiple-choice format to show that patients understand what they cannot otherwise produce. There are, however, important differences between the comprehension of such relationships and the spontaneous productions of the patient.

The paralogical defect goes beyond a logic or language disorder and involves other components of cognition, as in the parapraxis of catatonia, perceptual delusion, hallucinatory distortion, and dream. In each of these conditions, paralogic points to an incomplete semantic processing, or selection, of the emerging content and is, therefore, a clue to the impaired cognitive level.

The series of transitional forms that leads from schizophrenic language to word salad, which has been shown to correspond to an identical series in aphasic patients, is again repeated in the sequence uniting psychotic thought and dementia. Just as a functional psychosis may regress to a type of "organic" dementia, there is regression of organic dementia to a picture characteristic of "functional" psychosis.

DEMENTIA OF GENERAL PARESIS

This forms a link between psychotic thought disorder and organic (cortical) dementia. This intermediate position, and the tendency of the disorder to lean toward one direction or another, is a reason for the common confusion of diagnosis. Kraepelin (1913) described intellectual weakening, alteration of perception and attention, "clouding of consciousness," and recent memory loss. These features might suggest Alzheimer's disease, but there are also delusional elements and hallucination suggestive of schizophrenia. The memory disorder is not so profound as in Korsakoff syndrome; confabulations are of a grandiose nature and intermediate in certain respects between schizophrenic paramnesis (and systematized delusion) and the more banal substitutions of the true Korsakoff patient. The delusional formation is characteristic. The patient tends to elaborate on the most extraordinary, often tasteless, material—at times quite impressively—weaving a constantly changing story of unusual concepts and extravagant claims. The lack of systematization gives the impression that the train of thought is aimless and confused. There is impaired insight to the disease and poor correction of errors. Aphasic, apraxic, and agnosic symptoms are common in the course of the progression, leading ultimately to echo phenomena, grimacing, verbigeration, and terminal akinetic mutism.

An important analysis of paretic thought has been carried out by Paul Schilder (1951). Patients were studied for recollection of stories over time. Distortions in recall were similar to those in Korsakoff syndrome and schizophrenia in the affective transformation and the relation to the inner life, but they differed in that they were somewhat more commonplace. The wishes represented in the recall lacked the semantic complexity of those in schizophrenia. According to Schilder (1951) the schizophrenic thought disorder encroaches on the concept *in statu nascendi*, while that of the paretic attacks a relatively developed concept: "Each involves—so to speak—a different phase of the thought-process ... the schizophrenic's thought-disorder affects the core, the paretic's the periphery of experience."

The paretic stands midway between the schizophrenic and the true dement. The affective and delusional features point to the former; the disorientation, aphasia type, and memory loss suggest the latter. The confabulation is also of an intermediate nature. The transitional character of general paresis can, however, be better appreciated after a consideration of other organic dementias.

ALZHEIMER'S AND PICK'S DISEASE

Although these are usually not distinguished on a clinical basis, there are important differences in the presentation of these major forms of dementia. In Pick's disease, memory and insight can be relatively well-preserved for a period of time. Speech tends to be depressed, with word-finding difficulty and eventual mutism. In contrast, in Alzheimer's disease, there is a more rapid loss of insight and marked spatial disorganization. Language change leads from anomia to semantic paraphasia or jargon, while hallucination and/or paranoid ideation are common.

In Alzheimer's disease, the lack of insight and spatial defects point to the dissolution of representational level contents. Hallucination and semantic jargon indicate that the regression has reached the presentational (limbic) stage. At this point, a psychotic thought disorder appears. Thus, Rothschild and Kasanin (1930) described a case with incoherent speech: "If a person killing now, we ought to kill anymore; I never kill, try to save them and threw them into the weather." When she was asked why she was in the hospital, the patient said, "Yes, I forgot myself. My sister when she'd sit down she would say there's a string going up now. It's nice, but I go right up and fly with the fellows. . . ." The authors commented that their cases were similar to schizophrenia. Such patients are by no means rare. Schilder has noted frank psychotic episodes and delirium with mannerisms and stereotypies. In my own experience, this is a rather common observation in regressed Alzheimer cases.

Characteristically, in Alzheimer's disease, the progressive spatial disorganization leads to eventual loss of the external object, to a stage where the object is no longer "extrapsychic." This corresponds to the appearance of hallucination and semantic language alterations. Such patients may sit for hours talking to themselves unintelligibly in an evident hallucinatory state. A transitional stage is seen in which patients may converse with their own reflection in a mirror. This is a prelude to a wholly intrapersonal pre-object.

Although it is usually considered to be a late onset form of Alzheimer's disease, senile dementia appears to involve a cognitive level closer to general paresis. This is seen in the affective excitation, the nature of the confabulation, and the delusional trends. The more marked loss of recent memory and the confabulation led Alzheimer himself to consider the senile form as a separate entity. This combination of Korsakoff psychosis and dementia was termed *presbyophrenia* by both Wernicke and Kahlbaum. Some authors have treated presbyophrenia as a chronic form of Korsakoff psychosis. Delay (1962) noted a similarity in the memory defect but argued that the disorders were separable. The mood may vary from euphoria to irritability, though apathy is perhaps most common (Barbizet, 1964). Pathological studies suggest that the Korsakoff element may be attributed to a more pronounced involvement of the temporal lobes, which is consistent with a closer relation of presbyophrenia to limbic-stage disorders.

In Pick's dementia, the cognitive level of involvement is analogous to that of the more posterior forms, but it chiefly concerns the action component. Goldstein (1937) thought that the disorder interrupted a stage in advance of that in Alzheimer's disease, pointing to the relative preservation of more automatic performances. He argued that the language disturbance in Pick's disease concerned "the 'higher' functions of language, while in Alzheimer's disease, the 'speech material' is more deeply involved." According to Meyer–Gross (1938), the initial stages are characterized by a lack of affective control and jocularity (Witzelsucht). An early stage of hyperactivity may be followed by apathy and dullness. Memory and insight are spared for a longer time than in posterior dementias, and the spatial disability is not as prominent. The language change appears to consist of word-finding difficulty or reduced expression leading to eventual mutism. Echolalia and verbigeration are common.

The pattern of deterioration in Pick's disease is equivalent to that in Alzheimer's disease; the difference between them reflects a predominance of either the action or perception component of cognition. Both disorders begin at the level of generalized neocortex (as for example in word-finding difficulty) and regress toward limbic stage syndromes. In the more anterior disorder (Pick's), this regression appears in mutism and immobility, in the more posterior disorder (Alzheimer's), in hallucination and semantic jargon.

Comment

The various categories of dementia are not stable complexes of symptoms specific to each diagnostic form, but rather, within each form, there is an evolution over several cognitive levels. There are transitions between psychotic and paretic thought and from these to pre-senile dementia. Psychotic and paretic thinking reflect alterations at the limbic-presentational stage and lead, by way of presbyophrenia, to Alzheimer's disease, which initially involves the cortical-representational stage. The transition between these forms is marked by a progression from semantic disruption in language (e.g., paralogic) and an intrapersonal preobject (hallucination) to—or from—a stage of incomplete but relatively well-advanced content selection (concretism) with disruption of the extrapersonal object (spatial disorganization). These levels are also recapitulated with respect to the action development in Pick's disease.

The posterior transition is further marked by a systematic change in memory in which paramnesia, confabulation, and recent memory loss form a continuous series (vide infra). The change in memory, as well as in affect, occurs in relation to the constituent perceptual, linguistic, or action disturbances. Apart from these components, there is no external or restricted defect of thought. Paralogic, concretism, and abstract thought are ways of looking at these components in performance.

Abstraction refers to the ability to move from the particular to the category, or to elicit the category of (i.e., semantic field containing) two or more items. Deficits of abstraction occur in relation to perception as an inability to move between "depth" and "surface" stages in percept formation and in relation to language as an incomplete semantic realization of a particular content. *Concretism* is not just the absence of abstraction. The more prominent subjective element points to an earlier cognitive stage. In perception, performance has the character of an incompletely differentiated object; in language, concretism appears as a more preliminary phase of semantic development. A patient may achieve the semantic field of only one of several contents, in which the others are subsumed. In the deterioration of Alzheimer's disease, concrete thinking is a phase on the way to "associative" or paralogical errors. *Paralogic* is a special case or regressed form of concretism, just as the latter is a diminished form of abstraction. In relation to perception, paralogic appears in hallucinatory or imaginal fusions of a dream-like nature. Paralogical language occurs when one thing, say an object, is described through the semantic field of some related thing. The demonstration of a difference between concretism and paralogic depends in part on test methods. This is why the schizophrenic may show both forms of thinking. Whether the linguistic (or perceptual) product has demonstrable links to the intended response (as in "association") or whether those links are unrecognizable (as in word salad or semantic jargon) is determined by the "semantic depth" of the performance, that is, by the degree of semantic realization of a given content.

The concept of "overinclusion," which has been employed to explain schizophrenic thinking, is really a reflection of the spontaneous production of associative responses for choices within the semantic field of only one item. In this respect, there is no essential difference from paralogic. The term "association," however, does not adequately describe these responses since it wrongly suggests a sort of linkage or connection. Rather, the association reflects the nature of the semantic field of the presentation or, in spontaneous speech, of the intended (or demanded) response. It is an index of the configuration of items constituting a particular semantic field. The more "distant" is the response, the more preliminary is the semantic encoding of that performance.

MEMORY

What is the relation of memory to thought? A reminiscence is a kind of simple thought; a thought is a kind of complex reminiscence. The more a mental content inclines toward one or another of these activities, the more it is either a memory or a thought.

The reproductive aspect of memory has a counterpart in the process of thinking. When a thought is recurrent, we say that it is a recollection.

Similarly, a thought undergoes a process of growth. Is this growth or maturation to be attributed to thought or to memory? On the other hand, memory has a productive aspect. There is a new element in every recollection. A memory is never precisely true to experience but approximates it by degrees. To this extent, is the memory—the thought—also free from the experience.

We come to the conclusion that memory is a type of reproductive thinking and thought a kind of productive memory. Thus, to say that someone can think but cannot remember, or vice versa, is to say that he can think in one way and not in another. In both productive and reproductive thinking, there is a development. The nature of the content that emerges through this development determines whether it is to be called a thought or a memory. Reproduction is only one alternative in thinking.

If recall is simply another form of thinking, then a central problem in memory study will be that of retention. Retention and recall together constitute learning. How can we understand retention? Pathological studies indicate that more than just the reception and storage of a stimulus is involved, that what is retained is the complete microgenetic history of the experience.

Retention and recall also have an important relation to conscious state. An experience cannot be retrieved—that is, appear as a content in reproductive thought—in a microgenetic form in advance of that encountered during its registration. Childhood and hysterical amnesia, amnesia for dream and for hypnotic or other states of "altered consciousness," have in common the fact that the cognitive level realized during the original experience is microgenetically prior to that of the recall state. For this reason, the content of the earlier level is inaccessible, except during a state of cognitive regression (as for example in dream, hypnosis) back to the preliminary stage.

We may say that retention deals with an emergent pattern, not with a "bit" or a piece of an experience. The "store" or the "site" of the memory is the complete series of impressions left behind over all of the structural levels traversed by the original content. A pathological lesion of the brain, therefore, can disrupt this process at one or another stage but, barring total destruction of the cognitive structure, can never eradicate an experience once it has been deposited. For this reason, "loss of memory" does not imply a loss of some elements, but rather an alteration of recall due to a change in either the experiential or recall state.

Clinically, a distinction is often made between recent and remote memory. In pathological cases, recent memory is usually the first to be affected. In the "surface" cognitive disorders, such as early organic dementia, impaired recent memory reflects a dissolution retracing the ontogenetic sequence of deposition. The effect is not dissimilar to hypnotic age regression. Conceivably, the impairment in recent memory entails a facilitation in the recollection of distant events (cf. Shapiro *et al.*, 1956). This chronological aspect to memory and memory disorders can be understood in relation to ontogenetic stages of acquisition. As we have seen, intrahemispheric differentiation and the building up of more differentiated zones continues on into later life. This development has the effect of leaving prior experience behind in relation to a final cognitive stage that is continually being advanced. This explains the normal amnesia for childhood and, in the normal adult, may account for the superiority of memory for recent events. The course of "decay" in pathology is a reflection of these genetic relationships. In any event, the temporal aspect of recall (or forgetting) derives from an effect on the "trace"—as defined earlier—of a process of cognitive growth or dissolution rather than a change in the "trace" itself, as in theories of "consolidation" or "decay" of unconsolidated traces and so on.

Short-term memory refers to the more or less immediate reproduction of contents momentarily in consciousness. It is often tested in auditory perception by digit span or recall for other items serially presented. One can say that digit span is to recent or long-term recall as the eidetic image is to the memory image. Short-term memory is cognition given over to reproduction—in perception, action, or language. The product (e.g., the repeated digits) has not yet undergone assimilation; it has been modeled by, but has not yet become a part of, cognition. The capacity for such reproduction varies widely. Binet described a subject with a digit span in excess of 30, which increased to over 90 with rhythmic presentation. Such cases are comparable to eidetic prodigies. Impairment in immediate or short-term memory tends to occur in confusional states. The impairment is linked to a retrograde amnesia. In fact, a defect in short-term recall is the nucleus of a retrograde amnesia. The level of awareness is closely related to the capacity for immediate recall. This "level" is of central importance in both short-term memory impairment and retrograde amnesia. The retrograde defect occurs in relation to an alteration of awareness and is not bound to morbid states, for example, the amnesia for the brief period of time just before falling asleep at night.

There is no persuasive evidence that a different process is involved in short-term and long-term recall. Rather, cognition is looked at in a different manner. In the former, the process of perceptual formation is repeated in action, for example, in speech. There is a persistence of the original modeling that is not present in long-term recall. The decremental change in both duration and content recalled that is observed in the short-term period may well reflect—indeed, appears inversely related to—the sequence of phase transformations in cognition.

The various forms of memory disorder are determined by the cognitive stratum of the initial event and the level of pathological change. Each level incorporates a cognitive state to which recall is specific. As pathology proceeds "depthward," experiences specific to earlier stages become accessible to the lowered cognitive level. Impaired recall for recent events leads through a Korsakoff stage with confabulation. This may lead to a confusional dementia with inattention and impaired short-term recall. This level, achieved as an endstage in certain dementias, is the first stage of involvement in confusional states. The Korsakoff syndrome is intermediate between a dementia and a confusional state, appearing as a stage in the deterioration of the former and in the resolution of the latter.

Pathology of Memory

THE AMNESTIC SYNDROME

This appears in three major forms: following bilateral temporal lobectomy (hereafter, surgical amnesia), retrograde amnesia (e.g., posttraumatic), and Korsakoff's syndrome proper. In surgical amnesia, there is an impairment of memory going back for a period before the operation, that is, a retrograde amnesia, and a more profound learning defect after surgery (anterograde amnesia). The problem has been described after bilateral temporal lobectomy in an epileptic patient (see *Neuropsychologia* 1968 6) and in two cases with unilateral temporal lobectomy and pathology of the opposite temporal lobe (Penfield, 1974), and it appears to be similar to that seen in rare instances of bilateral temporal vascular disease, to the so-called "limbic encephalitis" as a remote effect of carcinoma, and to postherpetic encephalitis. The striking finding is the profound anterograde defect despite relatively normal performance on various tests of intelligence, speech, and perception. Characteristically, the patient is unable to recall that which he has just experienced, or he retains material only until his attention is shifted to another event.

Posttraumatic retrograde amnesia covers the period including and just prior to head trauma, often extending back several months or years. With improvement, the amnesia usually "shrinks" down to the period of impact. There may be islands of either recall or amnesia in the retrograde segment; an anterograde amnesia for the hospitalization is common. The disorder does not appear to differ fundamentally from other types of retrograde amnesia, as in electro-convulsive therapy, insulin shock, anaesthesia, and so on.

Korsakoff's syndrome refers to the occurrence of impaired recent memory, impaired learning, and confabulation in a patient with brain pathology. Descriptively, it is often considered as a surgical amnesia *plus* a dementia or *plus* confabulation. The involvement has classically been associated with lesion of the mamillary bodies, but recent work suggests the importance of medial thalamus (Victor *et al.*, 1971). It is seen not only in alcoholic patients but inter alia in tumor cases, postsurgically, or in other confusional states. Commonly, the Korsakoff psychosis begins as a confusional state and resolves into a confabulatory amnesia. In chronic cases, there may be an amnesia without confabulation. Mood may vary from apathy to euphoria, and the disorder may take on delusional features often of a paranoid type. Willanger (1966) has correctly stated that a psychological theory of the Korsakoff syndrome must account not only for the amnesia and confabulation, but also for the "asponteneity, lack of motivation, the vague field of experience and perceptual rigidity, and the strange, poorly adapted thinking."

There is a close inner relationship between these three amnesic forms. In fact, a continuum exists from Korsakoff psychosis to surgical to posttraumatic retrograde amnesia. The amnesic deficit following bitemporal lobectomy can enlarge (regress) into a Korsakoff syndrome, while the "shrinking" retrograde amnesia associated with head injury is a kind of mitigated or temporally isolated surgical amnesia. Surgical amnesia is not, however, the nuclear defect of Korsakoff's psychosis to which confabulation and an initial confusional state are added. Most likely, recall in the confabulating phase differs *qualitatively* from that in the chronic amnesic residuum, although the latter, apart from the dementia, is similar to surgical amnesia.

In these disorders, recall is not just deficient, but it is lawfully distorted. This is most clear in confabulatory recall. Betlheim and Hartmann (1951) have shown the relation of confabulation to mechanisms of the dream work; I have confirmed this finding in personal cases. Those patients without symbolic (semantic) distortion will be closer to surgical amnesia with improved insight and diminished confabulation. Moreover, if the recollections (confabulations) of the Korsakoff patient bear similarities to dream cognition, those of surgical amnesia have a similarity to normal dream forgetting. Thus, Milner's patient (H.M.) described his amnesia as: "You see, at this moment everything looks clear to me, but what happened just before? That's what worries me. *It's like waking from a dream;* I just don't remember [my italics]." A similar phenomenon occurs in posttraumatic retrograde amnesia as the defect in recall gradually resolves to a few seconds or minutes prior to the traumatic event. Islands of memory, not in precise chronological order, will appear as uncertain or dream-like recollections. Paramnesia is common during this stage, at times resolving out of a confabulatory state. The paramnesia gives way to a dim apprehension of the "memorandum," a kind of mnestic tip-of-the-tongue experience in which the affective content of the memory—as well as frustration at unsuccessful recall—are at an intense level. This finally leads either to full recall or to a restricted period of amnesia. A personal case illustrates this common sequence. This patient was involved in an automobile accident in which his fiancé was killed. As memory returned, there was increasing agitation and anxiety, particularly for events surrounding the tragic aspects of the accident. Disturbing dreams occurred prior to full recollection. One could say that the experience dominated cognition and the affective life prior to its recall.

To say that the amnesic syndrome reveals features of dream cognition is also to say that memory is not lost, but rather is only realized to a preliminary level. This is why Korsakoff patients may, in dream, produce fragments of the preceding day. There is also anecdotal evidence that, during recurrent Korsakoff bouts, recollection of the previous Korsakoff state survives in the new amnestic period. Patients with the amnestic syndrome are able to learn, but recall does not achieve a complete microgenetic development. It is an old observation that Korsakoff patients will refuse to shake hands with an examiner who has previously concealed a pin in his hand; although they give no verbal evidence of recall. This was even noted by Korsakoff: "A patient who disliked the (unrecollected) sessions of electrical (Galvanic) shock showed an ill humor on seeing the machine in spite of assurances that it was for the first time. We were able to see in his behavior the effect of a memory trace in his mind." Patients with surgical amnesia may also remember events of strong affective tone. The patient H.M. showed irritation and anger after the death of his father and ascribed this to an unrelated event. Later on he "seemed to be dimly aware of his father's death." The appearance in this patient of anxiety without recall is similar to that described earlier in the resolving retrograde amnesic.

In sum, the retrograde amnesia of the posttraumatic or electroconvulsive type is like the residuum of a confusional state isolated in subsequently normal mentation. Events of the amnesic period can achieve only that level of cognitive development realized during the original confusion (trauma). The brief period of retrograde amnesia that usually resolves out of the more extensive amnesic state may relate to the need for temporal context for the recall of specific items; that is, those contents emerging just prior to an abrupt alteration of cognitive level are deprived of normal temporal contextual relationships.

In surgical amnesia, there is impaired recall for events that are presumably experienced in a normal manner. Immediate recall is preserved. The disorder, however, is like a retrograde amnesia that is continually being renewed. In fact, this is the basis of anterograde amnesia; it is a retrograde amnesia in continuous formation. Aspects of these two disorders are again observed in the Korsakoff syndrome, as the patient resolves from a confusional state (i.e., a conscious level equivalent to that at the moment of trauma), through a picture having affinities to traumatic amnesia with confabulation (i.e., classical Korsakoff syndrome), to a chronic noncon-fabulatory state with a severe learning deficit.

CONFABULATION

This does not occur only in the amnestic syndrome, but also in a variety of neuropsychological and psychiatric disorders, such as in denial and hysterical states, cortical blindness, responses of so-called "split-brain" patients, and so on. In Korsakoff's syndrome, confabulation occurs pri-marily during the confusional prelude and the initial episodes and is less common in chronic cases. The symptom is often viewed as an attempt to "fill in a gap in memory," that is, as a type of compensation, a coping or denial mechanism, or as the reflection of whatever mnestic resources the patient has retained. Confabulation may concern recent events as well as those of the distant past and future, perhaps more prominently with "affectively charged" or illness-related material. It may be banal or witty, at times pretentious or even fantastic. The relation to dream thought has already been mentioned (see also K. Jaspers).

The acute Korsakoff syndrome commonly contains some disorder of language. According to Victor (personal communication), this consists of a "reduction in spontaneous speech, paraphasic errors in reading and writing and difficulty in recalling the name of an object (but not its use)." Other authors have noted a similarity of paraphasia in posttraumatic confusional states to schizophrenia (Curran and Schilder, 1935) and jargon aphasia (Patterson, 1944). In one carefully studied Korsakoff patient (Clarke *et al.*, 1958), semantic jargon coincided with florid confabulation, for example, as in the following response to the saying, "safety first": "I suppose it should mean to the ordinary person going up in education that it will mark your pen without any burn or flame or ink (perseverations from object-naming tests). You write on the paper with safety without any accident that might occur afterwards." In this patient, object naming was characterized by semantic paraphasia, for example, a cigarette lighter was referred to as "top hat lighter, asphalts and all that, tobacco accessory."

Confabulation is allied to the complex of semantic aphasic disorders. In the latter, the substitution is within the semantic field of the target lexical items, whereas, in confabulation, the semantic field itself—the concept—is substituted. Confabulation is also linked to paramnesia. According to Ey (1950), paramnesiae are "falsifications of the memory act which mix in the perception the past and the present, the real and the imaginary." This "mixing," however, may be an artificial element. The essential feature is that of substitution in recall. In this respect, paramnesia is comparable to paraphasia or parapraxia. The relationship between paramnesia and confabulation appears to be similar to that between semantic paraphasia and semantic aphasia, as between the referential and expositional modes. Confabulation would be a kind of *fluent* paramnesia in which isolated paramnesic recollections are serialized in continous speech.

In schizophrenia, paramnesia may show greater distortion with hallucinatory content. The confabulation of schizophrenic patients is often distinguished from organic cases by a lesser contact with the external situation; that is, schizophrenic confabulation is less adapted to, or influenced by, external events at any given moment. Thus the schizophrenic may give extravagant paramnesic accounts that appear to derive entirely from his imagination. In contrast, the confabulation of the Korsakoff patient can be manipulated by the interview. The confabulation of the posttraumatic amnesic tends to be centered on the traumatic event, that is, on the amnesic segment. This difference between the organic and functional case is, however, only apparent and reflects the "semantic depth" of the confabulation. The more the distortion there is, the more autonomous or subjective is the paramnesia, the deeper is the cognitive level. The confabulation in Korsakoff's syndrome points to a somewhat more superficial plane; thus, the paramnesia is closer to (i.e., seemingly more influenced by) the real world of the examiner.

This continuum between semantic jargon and paralogic, confabulation, paramnesia, and successful recall can occasionally be seen in a single case, in which there is a progression from initial semantic jargon as part of a confusional state, through confabulation proper, to a gradual restriction of the confabulation to the amnesic segments with the appearance of true paramnesia, and finally to either full recall or a stable amnesic segment. This transition is also accompanied by an evolution in affect and awareness. Finally, these "aphasic" features of amnesia correspond to "amnesic" features found in aphasia. This has not been fully appreciated since the aphasia tends to adumbrate all other elements on testing. The patient with semantic jargon, probably does have a type of embedded Korsakoff syndrome; generally after recovery he does not recall events that have occurred during the jargon state. This is probably also the case in schizophrenic patients who recover from a stage of word salad.

FUNCTIONAL AMNESIA IN RELATION TO THE AMNESTIC SYNDROME

A study of the amnestic syndrome has revealed close links to such "functional" phenomena as the forgetting of dreams and childhood experiences and hysterical amnesia. The amnesia for dream incorporates the entire sleep-dream duration in addition to the brief period of time just before falling asleep. On waking, these two elements merge in the retrograde amnesia. As in surgical and other amnesias, there is a sense of this duration, but the sleep time is not fractionated. The patchy recall of the retrograde period, the frustration at incomplete (but not utterly failed) recollection, and the rapid decay or fading time of dream contents interrupted by an awakening all have their parallel in organic states. Moreover, as in the organic amnesias, unretrieved contents are clearly "stored" but simply not recalled. The prior suggestion of continuity *within* repeated amnestic bouts in a Korsakoff patient calls to mind the speculation of William James concerning a continuity *within* separate dreams of contents shut off from the waking life. In this respect, the lack of a clear demarcation between the dream image and the dream thought should also be mentioned. Foulkes (1962) has shown that dreams have a history and a development as do waking thoughts. In fact, the constructive process of a dream is a kind of paradigm for—actually, a preliminary stage in—the constructive process of waking thought and memory.

Like dream amnesia, the forgetting of childhood experience has been explained through the repression attached to sexuality. It is held that the development of childhood sexuality is accompanied by feelings of shame, influenced by moral and social demands, and that this leads to a repression of childhood experiences. Similarly, in dream, forgetting is seen as an active process under the control of a censorship. Schachtel (1947), however, to whom we are indebted for the quote from Goethe that opens this chapter, has shown that the repression theory does not explain why nonsexual experiences are also prevented from reaching awareness; that is, why repression is so unselective. Rather, the amnesia for childhood can be understood as a consequence of the evolution of cognition to a more advanced stage, so that events of early childhood are—so to speak—"left behind" at a preliminary level in adult cognition. Amnesia for childhood and amnesia for dream are, respectively, consequences of the ontogenetic and microgenetic time course of cognitive formation.

In hysterical amnesia, there is "repression" of a traumatic event or fantasy. This repression is linked to the amnesia for childhood sexuality. In hysterical amnesia, the repressed content is more selective than in childhood forgetting. In fact, the nucleus of the hysterical amnesia is like the island of amnesia in a posttraumatic retrograde amnesia. The latter may even have symptoms that are not unlike those of hysteria. Hysteria, however, is concerned with earlier events in maturation. There is a more intense affective tone, and generally the amnesia has a more profound effect on adult cognition. The semantic distortion—and resultant symptom formation—that psychoanalysis has shown to be at the base of hysterical amnesia points to an "entrapment" of emerging cognitive material at the semantic level, either by virtue of its ontogenetically early, that is, "by-passed" or trance state, i.e. regressed, experiential level.

Theories of the organic amnesias tend to stress a decay of memory, a passive forgetting due to pathological destruction of the trace, while in the functional disorders an active process of repression is emphasized. In both the organic and functional series, however, the central problem is that some content is not available to the waking conscious life. This lack of "availability" points to the *state specificity* of the mnemic content. The fact that the contents of both organic and functional amnesias can be recovered during hypnotic or amytal-induced trance states is evidence for the specificity of recall to cognitive state (or level). It is an old observation that the contents of an otherwise forgotten epileptic aura can be recovered during a repeated attack. This can also be reproduced during intracerebral stimulation of the epileptogenic area. Overton has even shown that rats trained under amytal show no evidence of learning in the subsequent normal state but do show learning on reamytalization.

CORTICAL IMPAIRMENTS OF MEMORY

In this disorder, as in the organic dementias, there is generally an initial phase of forgetfulness that may persist for some time as a relatively isolated deficit. If there is some insight into the difficulty, there will also be a depression. Gradually, the amnesia for recent events—and perhaps in consequence, a preoccupation with events of the more distant past— becomes evident. As insight begins to fade, depression is replaced by apathy. In certain dementias, euphoria and/or mania may intervene. Word-finding difficulty and impaired spatial-constructional ability then appear; these defects all point to the level of generalized neocortex.

The pattern of memory loss in cortical dementia has been compared to the reduced learning capacity in normal aging. The latter, however, may not be a true deficit, but rather a by-product of continuing regional specification on into late life. If this is so, the amnesia of old age would be the paradigm for cortical amnesia, just as childhood amnesia is the paradigm for the amnestic syndrome.

A variety of other cortical pathologies will produce a memory disorder (see Whitty and Lishman, 1966). In all, the common element is an impairment in recall of recent events that may progressively encroach more and more upon distant memory and then upon immediate recall. With unilateral lesions, there is evidence for specificity as to verbal or visual recall. This has been repeatedly confirmed in patients with unilateral temporal lobectomy. It is of interest that Corsi (1972) has shown a relationship between the extent of the memory defect and the extent of surgical removal. It should be emphasized, however, that the memory defect following bilateral temporal lobectomy is in no sense a sum of the unilateral syndromes, the latter being relatively mild, often requiring special tests to be demonstrated. As with these temporal lobectomy cases, the "transient global amnesia" of Fisher and Adams (1958), whether ictal or vascular in origin, is also not a true neocortical syndrome, but rather it points to a limbic level involvement. The syndrome is a kind of encapsulated amnestic syndrome occurring in the course of otherwise normal cognition. The relatively normal behavior of such patients during the amnesia is undoubtedly similar to what Russell has termed "traumatic automatism" seen in cases of posttraumatic retrograde amnesia.

THOUGHT AND MEMORY

The Relation of Thought to Memory

We have seen that all thoughts or memories emerge through a selectional stage toward referential meaning. The goal of this process is an object, an action, or an utterance. With incomplete realization, characteristics of the formative process will appear in the product. The earlier is the stage in cognition to which these characteristics refer, the less is the distinction as to the thought or memory nature of the content. One can say that a thought that is not fully realized is like a memory that has slipped just beneath the surface of awareness. An hallucinatory distortion, a delusional paramnesia, a fantastic confabulation, and so on are both thought and remembrance according to how we look at them; they are thoughts to the extent to which they bring forth new content. Similarly, an amnesic segment has to do with memory when there are attempts at recollection and with thought when the amnesic material plays a productive role in cognition. These two dimensions of cognition—the productive and the reproductive—achieve expressions in the extreme in creative and mnemic genius (Chapter 9). Here we see that the creative is not a higher achievement but a step on the path to recall.

If memory is cognition given over to reproduction, then memory approaches thinking to the degree to which this reproduction is unsuccessful. Productive thinking is a deviation on the way toward reproduction: it is in some respects a kind of incomplete selection. In perception, this takes the form of an attenuation in the development toward an object, in language, as an alternative to reiteration. In both perception and language, the elicitation of novel form comes about as a feature of the semantic realization of content. Neither the thought nor the memory exists incipiently, as something in the background waiting to be expressed. After the thought or the recollection has appeared, we may look back and say that these were expressions of a deeper content, but this deeper content is only a more preliminary phase that gives itself up in the formation of the final "thought" or "recollection."

Memory is a constructive process in which a past experience serves in a sense as a goal. But how do we gauge the accuracy of this reconstruction?

Certainly the content of a perceptual experience is recalled more readily than that of an action or of an utterance. In the latter, reiteration is a type of productive recall. In perception, recollection arises in a repetition of the original perception. This may occur autonomously, as in an hallucination or memory image, or through a recurrence of the sensory incitation. Both types of perceptual recall, however, have a common substrate. The occasional uncertainty as to whether a recollection—or a recurrent perception—may have once been a dream or a real experience, as in déjà vu, arises because dream is a midway point in veridical perception. The degree to which the original perception is evoked in the act of recall may play a part in the judgment of the accuracy of reproduction but cannot serve as a standard against which this accuracy is judged. In action, there is also re-evocation of prior patterns, but here we are more inclined to speak of reiteration than of memory. These two phenomena—reiteration and recall—are not always distinguished in experimental studies that look only at behavior. Considered only as reproduction, memory is identical in both perception and action, but there is a difference in the subjective experience of recall. This derives from the different type of awareness experience generated by perceptual and action systems, since the awareness of the accuracy of a recollection is not outside the recollection but within the act of recollection itself, as a kind of product bound up with the recall state.

Amnesic Regression

In conditions in which there is a decay of recent memory not focussed on a fixed point in the past, amnesia and intellectual reduction occur together as part of the same regressive process. As reproductive thinking recedes to earlier levels, that is, toward "remote" memory, the memory deficiency gives way to a phase of elaboration. Cortical dements may show a transition from apparent "loss," to paramnesia and confabulation, to hallucination and delusion. Stages in this progression incorporate features of the paretic and schizophrenic thought disorders. At the same time, there is a transition from impaired "abstract thinking" to concretism and to "associative" or paralogical forms.

The organic disorders of productive thinking always entail a change in memory. There are, however, conditions in which memory is altered without an apparent change in thought. This concerns an amnesia that develops at a fixed point in time without progression, for example, posttraumatic retrograde amnesia, surgical amnesia, and various functional amnesic states. In such cases, the amnesic segment is comparable to an "isolated" content in the "split-brain" subject, where material is introduced (i.e., realizes the incomplete genetic level of) the right hemisphere (see Chapter 8).

On "Short-term" Memory and Later Recall

On tests of short-term memory, performance is always aided by meaning in the stimulus. Even in pathological states, such as echolalia, in which short-term memory is all that can be tested, as in repetition, the reproduction is not a simple copy of the stimulus but gives evidence of a development through cognitive stages. Studies of short-term memory utilizing both meaningful and nonmeaningful material indicate, from the point of view of response error, that semantic aspects of the stimulus come into play at successively greater intervals after presentation. Initial recall is true to the stimulus, and errors reflect its "physical" properties, for example, phonetic, morphologic, while later recall tends to be sketchy and related more to the general meaning of the presentation. These two classes of performance in short-term and long-term recall point to successive planes in cognition and not to separate mechanisms. The regression of a memory over time retraces stages in its cognitive realization.

The time course of decay in short-term memory seems to be linked to the phase sequence of cognitive formation. This is so even when the "trace" duration is attenuated by interference from competing stimuli. These "stimuli" point to new contents in cognition, that is, cognition given over to another microgenetic series. This decay time is probably linked to the final brief period of a residual retrograde amnesia.

What then becomes of the "short-term" content? Presumably every experience undergoing cognitive development is "stored," in the sense of a persistence of the hierarchic pattern of that developmental frame. The gradual incorporation of a perception into the mental life might come about through repeated but progressively more abortive evocations of the content. As the content becomes over time more "remote" from the present moment, it also recedes to a more preliminary stage and, consequently, to a more prominent role in *productive* thinking. This process also reflects, to an extent, the sustained growth of cognition to further levels. In later mentation, the assimilated content can lead: (*1*) to the construction of new form, that is, to productive, creative thinking, (*2*) to displacement, as in paramnesia, or (*3*) to partial or complete selection, that is, recall as in memory imagery. While this process of perceptual assimilation continues throughout life, there appears to be an evolution from an early stage in which cognition is dominated by perception to a stage in late life in which the assimilating content has a minor influence on an expanded cognitive structure. This change is reflected in behavior as early imitation leads to later habit and rigidity.

Microgenesis of Thought and Memory

The process of thought development can thus be reconstructed from the pathological. At an early stage, perception and action *are* the thought, *are* the memory. Memory and thought are not differentiated, and they find expression directly in behavior. As action, perception and linguistic contents emerge through the semantic level, opportunities are created for a divergence of the content from the path toward representation. In perception, the memory image and the object represent stages of more or less complete selection: the object "representing" (modeling) the stimulus, the memory image achieving a kind of self-representation. In lieu of the memory image and the object, certain of the emergent properties of perceptual development may come to the fore. Abstract and concrete thinking, and phenomena such as perceptual generalization, can be approached in this way.

When there is an abeyance of perceptual influence, cognition proceeds more or less autonomously. Memory and thinking can then be distinguished only by the final product. In a sense, thought is something that happens to memory in the course of its development. Memory becomes productive—becomes thought—when content undergoes growth rather than reproduction. One can say that thought is the product of forgotten memories. We have seen that, in pathological states, the amnesic content can exert a profound effect on thinking. This is true also of forgotten childhood experiences and of dreams. In such cases, "mnemic" content becomes "thought" content by a process of growth within the creative, form-building semantic layer. We do not mean solely linguistic by the term semantic. There is a form of thinking that does not require language. The importance of language in thinking is that language provides new content upon which the semantic operation can act.

Productive thinking is not the result of an "if . . . then" type of logic. Thought is not built up serially out of units but strives toward those units. Moreover, the logic within any utterance has the same status as the utterance itself. The logical structure of the syllogism, for example, cannot be taken as a model of thinking; in other words, logical structure is not there at the beginning determining or characterizing the thought but is something to be achieved. In order to know that an utterance is *true*, we must also relate the utterance to the microgenetic forms out of which it emerged. If one does this, for example, with the *Cogito*, one gets: "Thought occurs and the 'I' is embedded in—is a part of—the thought." The question of knowledge or existence is a separate matter about which the occurrence of thought says nothing, while the *ergo* is only an appeal.

All forms of productive thinking, whether in verbal logic, problem solving, play, or artistic thought, are creative in the sense that something new has resulted. This new something may take the form of a discovered common element in an otherwise puzzling or disparate group, or a progression may occur from a known element to the discovery of a group. We speak of *creative* thinking when the productive aspect of thought is very much in the foreground. Thought dominated by reproduction may be termed *iconic*. Genius refers to exceptional cases of creative or iconic thinking. Genius does not differ inwardly from normal cognition. In fact, what is true of genius will also be true of pathological thinking. Like pathology, genius can help us to understand cognitive structure

On the Psychoanalytic Theory of Thought and Memory

Fundamental to the psychoanalytic approach is the importance of the instinctual drives and layers of defense in the differentiation of the memory trace. Instinctual drive is conceived of as intensifying to the point at which, in the presence of a suitable object, there is discharge into motility or gratification. In the absence of an object, cathexis is transferred from the perception to the memory of the need-satisfying object, resulting in hallucinatory and somatic drive discharge. At this phase—the primary process—drive and idea are indivisible, and the perceptual object and the hallucinatory image are global and undifferentiated. This complex leads to the secondary process where there is an internally imposed delay in gratification. This delay permits a dissociation of the affective and ideational elements of the initial complex. The drive organization of memory gradually gives way to a reality—rather than wish—oriented process in which the final thoughts are determined by the censorship and by cathectic or energy distribution.

Of value in this account (after Rapaport, 1950) is the microgenetic formation of the idea and the concept of an increasing delay in discharge as a factor in thought formation. However, the notion of dissociation of drive energy and ideational content, the calling up of memories by energic diversions, the role of repression in the differentiation of ideas, these are purely artificial constructs that detract from the essential correctness of the genetic approach to thought development. The importance of energy mobilization and the consequent view of drive as something outside of thought necessitated a "motivational" theory based on the concept of gratification. The postulation of an energic process external to the idea is, in a genetic system, comparable to a claim of a directional force or power, or to an aim, an objective, in evolution.

Similarly, wish orientation in psychoanalytic theory refers to a stage of incomplete cognitive exteriorization and not to a content that is intrinsically "wish-like"; moreover, there is no contrasting principle of reality or reality orientation. Reality is not there beckoning cognition forward; reality is formed through layers of progressive differentiation. The primary and secondary processes of psychoanalytic theory incorporate two levels in the described series of cognitive transformations. The various subsidiary processes that have been proposed to account for this two-level system have, in the past, been viewed chiefly from the point of view of interpretation. It would be preferable to consider these processes, such as cathectic changes, hallucinatory substitutions, and so on, simply as *manifestations* at sequential levels in cognitive microgenesis rather than as contents in interaction.

7

Affect

We think of emotion as a *motive* force in behavior. This impression of our everyday experience is reflected in the account—the most influential in neuropsychology—of a primitive affective brain, that is, the "limbic system," acting on higher mentation and outward behavior. Implicit in this view is the idea of a center held in check by higher levels: The physiologist speaks of inhibition, the neurologist of release and control, the psychiatrist of repression.

Affect, is not an energy that invades and charges an idea at one or another level; it is not a force that moves among the memory traces of past events. Affect is not applied to cognition from without, rather it develops and changes—is *inwardly* present—at each level in cognition. Affect is like *form* to developing content. One can say that there is an affective side to every action, perception, or utterance.

126

Affect is the inner aspect of emotion, the latter being a more general term that includes display. Drive—instinct or instinctual drive—is a base-level affect from which the more differentiated affects—the feelings and moods—are derived. Emotions such as guilt or self-reproach, which figure in psychoanalytic theory, are so much a part of language that the affect is inseparable from its ideational content. We will not discuss these "affect ideas" since our concern is with patterns of affect formation and not with the finer differentiations.

According to Arieti (1967), the development of affect proceeds over three genetic levels. There is a progression from the proto-emotions, such as diffuse tension, motivation, appetitive behavior, and instinctual drive, through the intermediate paleo-emotions, which coincide with an imaginal stage in percept development, to the highest level of affect development, as in love, hate, and also perhaps in a primitive form of joy and depression. This concept of a genetic individuation of the affects over levels is retained in the proposed model although the sequence and designation of forms are somewhat different.

A Model of Affect Development

It has been proposed that affect, thus defined, undergoes a development in the same way that action or perception do, indeed, that action develops together with, or as another aspect of, action and percetion at each cognitive level, and that the various types of affect—the drives, anxiety, feelings—are to be understood not as mutually exclusive states or reactions, but as different levels in a unitary system of affect realization. Each of these levels is characterized by a certain affective tone, the specificity of which is determined by the relative emphasis on either the perceptual or action component at a particular moment in the cognitive flow (see Figure 6).

Sensori—motor cognition can be identified with instinctual drive. An instinct develops in relation to action and perception. If the development into an action predominates, the drive expression is into hunger; if the development into perception predominates, the drive expression is into sleep. Both hunger and sleep show a definite periodicity. Sexual drive seems to represent the phasic alternation or combination of these two

Structural Level	Affect Derivation	Stage in Cognition
Focal neocortex	Self-awareness	Symbolic
Generalized neocortex	Feeling (hate, love, depression, etc.)	Representational
Limbic	Anxiety (aggression, fear, and defense)	Presentational
Brainstem-hypothalamic	Drive (hunger, sexual, and sleep)	Sensori-motor

FIGURE 6. Stages in the derivation of the drives correspond to structural and cognitive levels.

(action and perception) drive forms. All three drive manifestations—hunger, sleep, and sexual drive—are centered around the body. The goal of the drive has not yet differentiated from an intrapersonal pre-object.

In man, states of excessive sleep and hunger may occur with lesions of hypothalamus. In animals, this can be induced by hypothalamic stimulation. The aimless restivity of some patients with deep midline lesions may correspond to the state of objectless motivation that characterizes the drive expression of hunger and sexuality. Catatonic stupor and motility psychosis may also fall into this category. There is a relation to arousal or vigilance. These represent drive as a stage in awareness (see Chapter 8).

The prominence of either action or perception tends to inactivate the other component. Sleep requires a suspension of motility. Hunger begins as an activity without an object. The object appears later, at which point the drive has also been transformed. This relationship between the drives can be observed in human infants, where the global drive state of hunger leads, in feeding, to rhythmic action, such as in sucking and associated body movements. This coincides with an attenuation of the drive and finally gives way to the opposite drive state, sleep, or satiation. These manifestations of instinctual hunger and sleep reappear later on in adult sexuality.

At the *limbic-presentational* level, there is differentiation within the developing base constituent of this drive organization. The "drive" nature of emotion is transformed to anxiety or tension. This is a fear or an apprehension associated with anticipation. The anticipation points to an incomplete object. As the affect develops with, and thus into, the forming object, there is a transformation of anxiety into partial expressions, such as anger and fear. These appear in the completion of the object development. Anger is the limbic transformation of the action-based hunger drive; fear is the derivative of the perception-based sleep drive. These affects re-appear in the limbic derivative of sexual drive as the complex of aggression and defense. Instinctual drive leads from appetitive states to the aggression complex through the mediation of predatory behavior. There are genetic links also between sleep and fear, for example, evasion, fear, or sleep paralysis, and there is evidence of displacement from one affect to another (Lorenz, 1965).

There is an association of emotionality with the limbic system. This is a result of the semantic transformation of content that throws the accompanying affective tone into relief. Affect is not discharged somatically as it is at a previous stage, nor is it directed at an object as in a subsequent stage. Affect is elaborated in a transitional space. This sets apart, and somehow intensifies, the affective component at this level.

The relation of aggressivity to temporal lobe lesions is well known. Fear and panic, anger, rage, and changes in sexual behavior have been described with lesion or seizure foci in the wider limbic system. Rage attacks occur on stimulation of human amygdala and occasionally with diffuse pathology. Pilleri and Poeck (1965) have observed a case of this type, with stereotyped outbursts of intense, low-threshold howling and teeth baring. This has been compared to experimentally induced "sham rage."

There are close relationships between the aggression: fear complex and laughing and crying. The study of experimental and pathological cases suggests a common structural organization, for example, a lesion producing rage in cat may give rise to explosive crying or laughing in man (Brown, 1967). Patients with bilateral lesions may burst into tears or sudden laughter, often denying an inner emotion appropriate to the display. Such outbursts are, however, generally triggered by a conducive setting, such as speaking to the patient in a sad voice or smiling. *This "pathological emotionality" is not the result of "release" of lower centers.* An affective state has occurred at a limbic level. The lack of concordance between the verbal report and the behavioral display is due to the fact that the display state and the "reporting state" refer to different (successive) cognitive levels. The well-known observation by Sperry (1967) of an affective response to a picture of a nude flashed tachistoscopically to the right hemisphere in a callosal-sectioned patient, a response subsequently denied or dismissed by the patient, is an example of a state- or level-specific phenomenon of this type. Similarly, panic or rage as an epileptic equivalent represents the coming to the fore of an earlier genetic level. The amnesia or lack of awareness for the behavior point to the inferior discharge level vis-à-vis subsequent waking cognition.

The limbic phase of language development brings about a change in the aggression: fear complex. This results in a type of elation and in apathetic or morbid depression. Euphoria is common. Paranoid behavior provides a link between euphoria and aggression.

Though associated with frontal lobe pathology, euphoria is present in a variety of conditions with lesions outside the frontal lobe, such as denial, Korsakoff psychosis, and jargon. The relation to semantic processing is evident in the lack of insight that often accompanies the euphoria. Mania is a kind of agitated euphoria, a euphoria in relation to anxiety.

In conversion hysteria, there is a bond between euphoria and indifference (*belle indifférence*). This euphoric indifference to a conversion symptom is related to the euphoric denial of a hemiparetic limb. Hysteria reflects a symptom formation at a semantic stage, as does denial. The hysteric admits the deficit, since the level of the incompleted content generating the euphoria is only a small part of his cognition. In organic denial, all cognition may regress to the earlier stage. There is also a close relationship between organic denial and the Korsakoff syndrome.

In morbid depression, there are feelings of passivity, unreality, and depersonalization. This passivity and emptiness point to a dissolution of the object world. Agitated depression occurs as a phase into or out of a morbid depression, when the object loss is incomplete. Irritability or anger appear as an orientation toward the world. We see the position of anxiety in anger and depression according to the action or perception bias.

In schizophrenia, there is usually an absence of anxiety. Anxiety is considered to enter the picture only secondarily, as in agitation or paranoiac fear. Anxiety, therefore, is a stage that is near to the attainment of the object. In psychosis, it signals an improvement. Similarly, anxiety may accompany stages in the resolution of a retrograde amnesia.

The *cortical-representational* level achieves a fixed external world. There is a radiation of affect out into the objects of that world. Affects are in relation to objects. The affect will have less immediacy; it does not lead so precipitously into a display pattern. The ideational aspect of the affect is more prominent. The affect settles around this emerging ideational or linguistic content and gives rise to more highly individuated feelings and moods. The affect also proceeds outward with action and perception, exteriorizing and thus building up the affective life of objects. The closer relation to the external object, the mitigation of the display, and the "empathetic" nature of object relations, are common aspects of the neocortical level.

Love and hate are feelings that are derived from anxiety and the fear–aggression complex of the preceding level. Love is the feeling generated by the affect flow out into that object. There is a state of complete empathy. Empathy is one expression of love. Hate occurs when that affect flow is threatened with loss. Love and hate appear in the gain and loss not of objects, which are joy and depression (or grief), but of the affective life of objects.

There has been little study of the consequences of organic lesion on affective realization at this level. The most prominent changes are frustration and a type of apathetic depression. Frustration coincides with a dawning awareness of content (and error), depression with an intimation of an object loss. Both frustration and depression can dissolve into anxiety and catastrophic reaction as a regression to an earlier cognitive level. Frustration and apathy are also in relation to the volitional attitude and indicate the affective basis of consciousness.

The final *symbolic* stage in affect development would seem to lead to such distinctively human emotions as guilt, faith, humiliation, and so on, where the ideational or linguistic component is in the foreground. These affects or "affect ideas," are linked to the preceding level. The affect is dissipated as the idea reaches a level of verbalization. The awareness that accompanies this verbalized affect is the sole affect derivation at the symbolic level (see Chapter 8).

If the idea is similar to the inner experience of the utterance, then feeling is similar to the inner experience of the idea. Idea and feeling do not exteriorize themselves in the same manner as do perception and action. Feeling persists as an inner experience, while the idea seems to be an expressive content that is detached from its affective tone. This phenomenon gives the false impression that affect and idea undergo a separate fate in development. Pathological involvement at this level will have the effect of a passivity to the world, loss of will, and reduced self-awareness.

Comment on the Psychoanalytic Theory of Drive

The psychoanalytic concept of drive as force or energy developed out of an attempt to account for disorders, such as conversion hysteria and obsessional neurosis, on a common basis. Drive came to be conceived as a kind of pressure or a quantity that could be added to or subtracted from memory traces and ideas. The varied expressions of drive and its final derivations were conceived of as points or stations in a discharge pathway. Subsequently, a distinction was made between sexual and self-preservative or ego instincts, and a pivotal role was assigned to narcissism in drive individuation. Concepts, such as hypercathexis, decathexis, and affect quotas, lead to a considerable elaboration of what was originally quite a simple model.

The fundamental problem with this view concerns the dissociation of drive and idea. Drive was banished from cognition and became an external element. The failure of a content to develop signified either a censorship from above or a withdrawal a tergo of motive force. This gave rise to a structure of defenses imposed upon an otherwise productive system of drive derivations. In other words, it led to a "conflict" theory of drive manifestations. Conflict, however, is itself a manifestation of affect and not a mechanism, in its differentiation. The "viscissitudes" of instinct—drive, affect, and feeling and their varied expressions—are not the source or the product of intrapsychic conflict, but they are simply ways of characterizing the different components of cognition at successive levels of realization.

There is no need for the concept of psychic energy (instinct, motivation) as a motivating force in cognition. The orderly sequence and unfolding of cognitive levels repeats and extends the phylogenetic and ontogenetic pattern. The progression from depth to surface, the incessant repetition of developmental form, and the striving toward higher levels are all part of an evolutionary trend that leads in a forward direction *simply because it is in the nature of the organization to unfold in this manner.*

Affect and Cognition

Instinct is not lost in human cognition in the course of evolutionary advance, but rather it gives rise to affect derivations that lack instinctual features. To demonstrate instinct in behavior, cognition must express itself at a level prior to these derivations. The direct global discharge in perception, for example, "releasers," and in action, for example, "consummatory response," as seen in animals is their cognitive endpoint. In man, this is a transitional phase. The releaser is not yet an external object; the response is not yet a differentiated action on that object. Further development of these components will carry the performance away from instinctual features.

We have described three instinctual drives: hunger, sleep, and sexual drive. These develop in relation to action and perception: hunger reflects a bias toward action, sleep toward perception, and sexual drive a base level discharge of both components. Each drive has a periodicity. This is important in determining which drive will appear. Both hunger and sexual drive begin with an intrasomatic source and proceed toward an extrapersonal object. The satisfaction of these drives allows sleep—the sleep drive—to come to the fore. If drive is not immediately expressed, it is either displaced to another base level drive, which then seeks expression, or it is transformed to subsequent cognition. Expression then comes about through the affect derivative of that drive at the higher cognitive level.

Each base-level drive has a derived affect at each level in cognition, and all of these affects are recapitulated in the expression of each drive category. For example, in sexuality, the base-level drive leads outward to the distant object and, ultimately, to the feeling of love. In sexual union, there is a withdrawal back to the base-level drive. Affects at intermediate levels, such as anxiety and the aggression—fear complex, come into play in both the outward and regressive directions. Love represents the endpoint of the differentiation of sexual drive which then dissolves, in sexual union, back to an initial stage of rhythmic action about the axial musculature and pre-object—even hypnic—features in percept development.

Anxiety points to an incompletely developed or dissolving stage in action or object formation. Bias toward either of these components alters anxiety in the direction of aggression or defense. The transformation of hunger through food acquisition into aggressive behavior corresponds to a transition between sleep and fear paralysis. Without such bias, or when the development is in some manner distributed over both components, drive is transformed to sexual anxiety. The *Aktualneurose* may refer to pathology at this level.

Sexual behavior incorporates level-specific aggressive and defensive elements. This establishes a linkage to the derivations of the other base-level drives. The transition of sexual drive from an oral-hypnic organization to one centered in aggressive—defensive behavior corresponds to analytic concepts of the latency period. Latency, however, is not the result of conflict (repression). It is an *achievement* by sexual drive of a more advanced level of differentiation.

Affect moves outward in the attainment of the object. Affect differentiates with and objectivizes in the object. The object is not "charged" with affect; the affect is not "attached" to the object. Both develop together as different aspects of the same process. As the object emerges from the pre-object field, it changes as it receives (draws out) more and more of the affective life. Like objects, affects must be continually renewed. This inner relationship between object and feeling, which is not as prominent when affect is distributed over the everyday world of perception, comes to the fore when an object-bound affect is experienced strongly. When we see someone with "eyes of love," we see them differently qua objects. The space of an object that is loved is not the same space as that of other objects. This change in the object and the change in the feeling state do not condition one another but are simultaneous occurrences.

Moreover, the object that is gained can also be lost. In depression, anxiety occurs as the object is about to be lost or as a phase in recovery. Depression in organic or psychotic states signals an imminent loss of the object world. Here the object and its accompanying affect cannot be drawn back into a world of other objects as is the case when the loss of one object—as in bereavement—is the basis of the depression.

Affect also moves outward in relation to language. The affective core of the utterance is seen in obscenities or in concepts such as God or patriotism. The affective value of words is comparable to that of such affect ideas as guilt. These refer to the cortical-representational level just beneath the surface of introspection. This is why, in psychoanalytic therapy, the verbalization of the affect has a helpful effect: not through discharge but through transformation of the affect to the symbolic level. The self-awareness that characterizes such verbalization *is* the affect derivation. The affect leads in two directions: outward with the final utterance, as into the objects of the preceding stage, or with idea to form self-awareness.

In this final derivation to self-awareness, the affect loses its "affective" character. The emotional core of the affect has been "left behind" at the representational stage. Feelings that can be referred to language are drawn into this affective endstage. The feeling of passivity in perceptual development, which accompanies the exteriorization of the object, is heightened during states in which the image is the focus of consciousness. In linguistic introspection, the active attitude of action development is accentuated into a belief in "self" as agent. Affect becomes finally a kind of faith in the self as both receiver and actor in the world.

8

Consciousness and Volition*

*He hath set the world in their heart,
yet so that man cannot find out the work
that God hath done from the beginning even to the end.*

Ecclesiastes

In general, we may say that awareness is not a state or an attitude attached to performance but has a developmental character. Piaget has commented that awareness in the young child begins, not as an "awareness of objects" or an "awareness of activity," but rather as an undifferentiated state out of which more highly developed levels emerge. Because of this developmental character, it is difficult to give a definition or description of awareness as such, since the various manifestations of awareness, for example, vigilance, wakefulness, arousal, attention, set or orientation, self-awareness or consciousness of, refer to different *levels* in a unitary formative process rather than to independent mechanisms.

*Published previously in Brown (1976) and reprinted here with revisions through the courtesy of Plenum Press, New York.

Not only does awareness develop over several levels, but, at each level, awareness occurs as an inner part of the cognitive stage associated with that level. Awareness is another aspect of the microgenesis of action, perception, and language, and it differs according to the developmental stage of these components. This is why it is misleading to say that a content *enters into* consciousness or that one is or is not conscious *of* a particular content. This gives the erroneous impression that consciousness seizes the content from outside or that the content gains access to consciousness. The content is as much *in* consciousness as consciousness is *in* the content. In addition, like the content, consciousness is also a momentary achievement, a kind of product that needs to be continuously renewed.

Introspection refers to a consciousness of a content: *consciousness of.* The idea of consciousness of, however, does not necessitate the logical possibility of a series of compounded introspective states. Consciousness of refers to a real psychological event. The idea of a consciousness of that consciousness of comes from a false understanding of consciousness as something external to the content. The opposition between consciousness and content, which seems to be implicit in consciousness of, is, in fact, the mode of presentation of the conscious state and not an aspect of its underlying nature. In this respect, Brentano (1874) has written: "The consciousness which accompanies the presentation (of a sound) is a consciousness not so much of this presentation as of the whole mental act in which the sound is presented, and in which the consciousness itself exists concomitantly."

It may fairly be asked whether planes of awareness exist between a consciousness of objects or of activity and true introspection. Ontogenetic studies suggest a gradual transition from one level to the next. The evidence from pathological cases also seems to point in this direction, that is, to a series of levels in a continuum and not to a sharp quantal break between radically different forms. One cannot, however, apprehend states of consciousness in oneself other than the immediate state; in other words, the state can only know itself. For this reason, prior levels may be misrepresented as nonconscious, rather than as primitively conscious. The concept of an ascending series of levels of consciousness avoids, to some extent, this problem (i.e., whether consciousness is a product of primitive consciousness or of a nonconscious state) since the problem results from the idea of consciousness as extrinsic to content and the consequent importance of consciousness of as the sine qua non of any conscious state.

The existence of preliminary forms of consciousness can be inferred from the behavior of patients. Since only the final stages of consciousness are readily accessible through private introspection or interrogation of others, earlier levels must be reconstructed from the pathological material. Our most objective means of achieving this reconstruction is through the use of behavioral and verbal performance, but even here research into the nature of the preliminary stages is largely intuitive. Even the private recollections of dreams may not adequately represent the experience of the dream state since the latter, to achieve inrospection, has passed on to a further genetic level; that is, the introspected content is realized to a level beyond that which is taken to be the object of the introspection. We can no more be sure that what is recalled of a dream is a faithful copy of the actual dream than that our consciousness of, the state of introspection, is the endstage of cognition. In dream, there is no awareness of the subsequent (waking) level. The dream state is a closed system of reality, a universe. Upon waking, there is merely a dim apprehension of the preceding stage, which is possible only because the latter gives rise to (indeed, is necessary as a part of) the introspective level. Yet like dream, introspection is also a closed system. We cannot even guess at what conscious forms might lie beyond.

LEVELS IN CONSCIOUSNESS FORMATION

Awareness refers to the configuration of components within a particular cognitive level. It is this configuration that determines the constitution of the awareness state. If one could specify everything about these compoents, that is, about action, perception, and language at a specific level in cognition, the total phenomenal realization of these specifications would constitute the awareness experience.

We have said that affect is the form or configuration of the content of a particular component at a particulr cognitive stage. From this, it follows that there is a close relationship between affect and awareness. Awareness is the form of all components at a given moment at one level in cognition. In a sense, therefore, awareness can be identified with the total affective content; that is, awareness is the affective aspect of all components simultaneously.

Affect and awareness *seem* to have a reciprocal relationship. From the genetic point of view, however, this apparent reciprocity is a sign of an inner identity. Intense affective states do not preclude consciousness (in the sense of consciousness of); the affective state *is* the consciousness experience at that particular level, the affect pointing to a stage at which consciousness of does not yet exist.

If affect is the *experience* of consciousness, then the *content* of that experience is determined by the primary components. For example, the degree of perceptual realization will determine whether consciousness is organized about the dream state or the object world.

Four levels—arbitrary phases—in consciousness formation can be distinguished that correspond to the described cognitive stages. *Sensori-motor* cognition would be characterized by an action series ranging from simple wakefulness or arousal to states of drive or motivation and a perceptual expression in dreamless sleep. The immediacy of the performance and its enactment within a single, probably atemporal, somatic space field would not permit a "private" experience. Indeed, in a sense, the behavior *is* the private experience. A comparison with pathological conditions of the same structural level, such as coma or coma vigil, is suggestive. In the *limbic* stage, developing intrapersonal space both extends and begins to "fill in" the consciousness experience. The semantic transition of this level does not yet permit an object consciousness, but the emergence of forming (isolating) contents achieves the initial step of an "opposition" between these various contents, as well as between the level and the prefigurating ground. Dream and psychotic hallucinosis and partial expressions, such as derealization or depersonalization, are manifestations of this level. The *neocortical* level achieves a stable object world. The organism perceives and acts in that world. This object or action consciousness is directed outwards, because the exteriorization of the object has "left behind" an intrapersonal component that is not yet a parallel formation. For this reason, the intrapersonal, the self, cannot yet serve as an object for cognition. At the *symbolic* level, consciousness of self (consciousness of intrapersonal content, not self-recognition) is achieved by means of language. This occurs through the cognitive advance accompanying language production, and it concerns a progressive articulation by language of a new intrapersonal space developing against (out of) the exteriorized space of the "outside world" and apprehended as intrapsychic. The articulation of this new space occurs through a kind of objectivization of intrapersonal content beyond that already achieved in the formation of the extrapersonal object.

Although language recapitulates earlier stages in action and perception, it does not seem to contribute uniquely to the formation of consciousness at these early levels. The utterance, however, is an important means of access to preliminary stages in the private world of consciousness. In pathological states, the utterance is a representative of preliminary cognition and, thus, of the consciousness elaborated at that stage. In organic cases, this can best be studied in disorders in which the alteration of consciousness, in relation to language, is in the foreground of the clinical tableau: hemispheric disconnections (the so-called "split-brain" model), denial syndromes, aphasia, and confusional states.

The Split-Brain Model of Consciousness

Following surgical section of the human forebrain commissures, special testing of patients has suggested a separate awareness experience restricted to events occurring within each hemisphere. The evidence for this interpretation, which is of great importance to contemporary study of the nature of consciousness, is so well-known that the reader is simply referred to two recent monographs (Gazzaniga, 1970; Dimond, 1972) and to the paper on consciousness by Sperry (1969).

Characteristically, a "callosal" patient (with eyes closed) is unable to name objects placed in his left hand. Generally the patient does not say "I don't know," but he either does not respond at all or, more commonly, gives paraphasic or confabulatory answers. For example, a patient of Sperry's called a pencil held in the left hand a "can opener" and a "cigarette lighter"; a patient of Geschwind and Kaplan (1962) identified a ring in the left hand as an "eraser," a watch as a "balloon," and a screwdriver as a "spoon" or a "piece of paper." If the patient is then asked to select with the left hand the (still unseen) object from a group of objects, he will tend to select—if it is present—the object named in the confabulation. Thus, if a key has been placed in the left hand and identified verbally as a comb, the left hand will select the comb from the object group. If the procedure is repeated nonverbally, the correct object is selected. I have also observed this phenomenon in personal cases. We see that the "left hemisphere" confabulation determines the left hand ("right hemisphere") response. Moreover, the patient appears to be not only unaware of "right hemisphere" events, but also of the erroneous nature of the misnaming, which is a product allegedly of the left hemisphere.

This failure of the patient to admit a lack of awareness for experiences presumably restricted to the right hemisphere is only one indication that *the stimulus object has undergone bihemispheric processing.* The confabulation is also a sign that an object has developed in both hemispheres. The lack of awareness for the erroneous nature of the confabulation reflects the fact that the object name is realized in right and left hemisphere only to a semantic level. The response, the confabulation or paraphasia, is comparable to the semantic paraphasia of standard aphasics, in which there is also a lack of awareness for the incorrect performance. This verbal response in the left-hand test situation, for example, "eraser" for ring, is proof that the content has developed to an intermediate stage in *left* hemisphere. Moreover, the nature of the paraphasia, whether categorical or asemantic, will reflect the degree of microstructural development within left hemisphere, a level that is determined by, and is continous with (i.e., part of the same ground as), right hemisphere language capacity. This capacity is, in turn, related to the degree of lateralization which varies from one individual to another (Brown and Hecaen, 1976).

The correct nonverbal identification or selection of the object with the left hand and not with the right hand points again to the state-specific nature of the performance and not to a separate hemispheric localization or "lack of transfer." The *endstage* cognitive level of the successful "right hemisphere—left hand" performance is continuous with an *intermediate* stage in left hemisphere. Therefore, the performance (cognitive) level of the patient in the right-hand—left-hemisphere situation represents a stage beyond that to which the content has been processed in right hemisphere, even though this processing achieved a correct "nonverbal" response. In other words, the correct "right hemispheric" selection corresponds to a content in left hemisphere that is pre-terminal to the actual performance level. In this regard, one should emphasize that the lack of a verbal element in the test situation, that is, so-called "nonverbal" matching, does not indicate that the performance occurs exclusively through nonverbal systems. The absence of the verbal element is an absence on the test *and not in cognition.*

According to this analysis, *the hemispheres act as one* up to a certain cognitive stage that will vary according to the degree of lateralization. Beyond this level, asymmetric structures carry cognition to a further level in one (the left) hemisphere only. There are several clinico-pathological disorders that confirm this interpretation of the surgical material. One such disorder is the left-sided (so-called "sympathetic") apraxia that occurs with left frontal lesion, usually in the presence of a right hemiparesis and some degree of aphasia. The condition has been attributed to an interruption of fibers passing from left to right frontal region concerned with movement of the left side in response to verbal command. The explanation is, therefore, much the same as that advanced for left-sided apraxia after surgical section of the corpus callosum. The nature of the impaired performance, however, is quite different in the two conditions. In the former, there are clumsy or dyspraxic approximations to the target action, while in the surgical cases, action is dextrous but is more or less unrelated to the command. In "sympathetic" apraxia, the action pattern is more advanced in its development and, therefore, closer to the goal. The awareness that accompanies this action is also more developed, and thus there is some recognition of error. In the surgical case, the action pattern points to a more preliminary stage. The dislocations or parapraxes reflect a semantic level in the developing action comparable to the semantic level of the confabulatory misnamings discussed earlier, and, as in confabulatory misnaming, the incorrect performance, the action, is not accompanied by full awareness of error.

One can make an identical set of observations in the condition of agnosic or "pure" alexia. This disorder occurs with lesion of the left occipital lobe and splenium of corpus callosum. There is a right visual field defect. The central feature of the disorder is an impairment of reading in the intact visual field, that is, in the "right hemisphere." The classical interpretation is identical to that of the left visual field alexia in the surgical patient, namely, an interruption in the flow of written material from minor (right) hemisphere to language areas on the left side. However, closer attention to the reading difficulty in these two forms indicates that this common explanation is incorrect.

The reading difficulty in the clinical case contrasts with that of the surgical patient. Most patients with agnosic alexia can read single letters and can construct simple words through a process of letter-by-letter spelling. Errors in reading tend to reflect morphological relations to the correct words. There is awareness of error and some degree of frustration. In contrast, words flashed briefly in the left visual field of the surgical case evoke confabulatory and paralexic readings. While the former patient might read the word *chair* as "chase," showing a closer approximation to the target item, the surgical patient might say "throne" or "sofa" or give a confabulatory answer. Moreover, readings in the surgical patient are more facile and effortless than the slow, labored readings of the agnosic alexic and are not accompanied by such an acute awareness of error.

These differences between the surgical and clinical patients in disorders of action (apraxia) and perception (alexia) represent the extremes of a range of performance in which all grades of transition occur, both from moment to moment in testing, as well as from one patient to another. These transitions are an indication of the momentary "depth" of the performance, that is, whether it is closer to the semantic level, as in paralexia or parapraxia, or to the final (target) action or perception. Moreover, in these transitions, one also observes a change in awareness of content, as well as of affect, such as euphoria becoming frustration. These findings indicate that the performance of such patients reflects the genetic level achieved by a particular content in cognition and not its hemispheric isolation. Indeed, within the extremes of performance illustrated by the clinical and surgical patients, one can find a wide array of aphasia symptomatology. Such cases support the view that awareness is specific to cognitive stage and that instances of what appear to be separate awareness point instead to multiple levels in a unitary process.

The Syndrome of Denial

Denial or lack of awareness of disease (anosognosia) is a common manifestation in both organic and functional disorders. The first description was by von Monakow (1885) with respect to two cases of cortical blindness, while the term anosognosia, often applied to this phenomenon, was coined by Babinski (1914) with respect to lack of awareness of hemiparesis. Lack of awareness is also characteristic of several aphasic forms, such as jargon, stereotypy, and echo responses. In general, three types of denial are recognized: partial or incomplete awareness of a deficit; explicit denial of the deficit or, in the case of hemiplegic denial, of the very existence of the hemiparetic limbs; and denial associated with distortion, hallucination, or other illusory phenomena referrable to the impaired body zone (e.g., phantom or reduplicated limbs, visual hallucination).

The view that denial is a reaction of the personality as a whole to the disorder is contradicted by the selective nature of the symptom. Thus, patients with left hemiplegia may deny weakness in the arm but admit to weakness in the leg. This occurs when there is a return of threshold sensory or motor function in the lower extremity while the arm remains fully paralyzed. Similarly, there may be catastrophic depression over subtotal cortical blindness with persistent denial of a hemiplegia. One patient with a left hemiplegia and previous amputation of the first two fingers of the left hand was able to correctly explain why he could not move his amputated fingers, but, when asked to move the other (paralyzed) fingers of the same hand, he refused to admit the paralysis. Stengel (1946) described a case of cortical blindness with denial of the totally blind right visual field and awareness of visual loss on the left side where only minimal vision remained (motion and light perception). Thus, denial may spare a less recent disorder, may involve one of two (usually the more severely involved) hemiparetic limbs, and may spare deficient performances that relate to the same body zone depending on the reason for the deficiency.

In patients with denial, there is commonly some degree of disorientation, recent memory loss, and a confabulatory trend. There appears to be a relationship between the severity of the perceptual deficit and the confabulation. Cases of denial with fair visual or somaesthetic perception will have a marked Korsakoff syndrome. On the other hand, the more severe the perceptual impairment is, the less prominent need be the Korsakoff and confusional state. In those cases in which confabulatory denial is accompanied by hallucination in the impaired modality, such as visual hallucination in patients with cortical blindness, the hallucination, like the confabulation, should not be viewed as a cause of the denial, but rather as a manifestation of the same level of disruption.

An interpretation of denial begins with the view that *awareness of a content is always related to the microgenetic level achieved by that content.* A somaesthetic or a visual percept is, therefore, not outside of awareness but is realized—with the awareness form bound to that content—only to an incomplete stage. Thus, when a cortically blind patient claims that he can see (the so-called Anton's syndrome) he is, in fact, correct, although his perception, and the awareness for that perception, are at a pre-object level. Moreover, the confabulation that characterizes many such patients also points to a preliminary level and, in this respect, is comparable to the confabulatory naming of "split-brain" patients to objects in the left hand or visual half field.

Language and Awareness

There are three major forms of aphasic language that are characterized by deficient insight: the stereotypy, the echo response, and certain forms of jargon speech, including semantic paraphasia.

The stereotypy or recurrent utterance is a feature of Broca's and global aphasia. The utterance may consist of single words, such as "yes," "no," or "fine," oaths or profanities, brief phrases, such as "Oh my God," or a few words in unintelligible jargon. There is an important difference between stereotypic and volitional speech. Stereotypies are well-articulated, show brief latency or explosiveness, and often show preservation of speech melody, stress, and intonation. During the utterance, the patient may be excited or euphoric and gives no evidence of awareness of the stereotypic content. In contrast, the volitional speech of a patient with stereotypic utterance is slow, labored, and dysarthric with acute self-awareness and frustration. Moreover, patients who recover from a Broca's aphasia do not recall the stereotypic content but may painfully recollect their initial attempts to produce their own name.

A transition occurs between the stereotypic and the volitional utterance. The stereotypy evolves from complete automaticity without awareness, through modification and then blocking, which is at first partial and incomplete. At a later stage, the stereotypy may alternate with some volitional speech; finally, the complete inhibition of the stereotypy signals the return of volitional speech.

There is some tendency to attribute the stereotypy to the action of right hemisphere, given a lesion on the left side. The stereotypy, however, is not a phenomenon in isolation but undergoes a gradual change with the return of volitional speech, nor is the stereotypy sharply differentiated from awareness. It is neither the residuum of damaged left hemisphere nor the highest vocal achievement possible in the intact right hemisphere, but rather the result of both acting in unison at a preliminary language level.

There is a close relationship between the stereotypy and the echo reaction. Echolalia is also a brief-latency, well-articulated, often explosive iteration without awareness seen in focal aphasic disorders as well as in diffuse organic states. The short, one to two word echolalic repetitions of the posterior (jargon) aphasic are, in fact, exactly analogous to the stereotypies of the anterior patient. When both posterior *and* anterior regression occur, the result is echolalia and stereotypy as a more or less isolated feature of language performance, the so-called "isolation syndrome" (see Brown, 1975b, for further discussion).

Echolalia is clearly not a simple audio–verbal reflex but, like the stereotypy, is in relation to other language performances. Thus, echolalia occurs only when the patient is addressed. There is personalization of the iteration (e.g., when asked "How are you?" the patient responds "How am I?"), and, given incorrect presentations, the patient produces a correct grammatical form. Moreover, there is often a relationship between the fidelity of the repetition (the echo) and the degree to which it is understood. Patients may show echolalia for nonsense words or a foreign language and paraphasic repetition for the mother tongue. In some patients, one can see a transition between the echo and normal repetition. This transition takes place over four stages: (*1*) initial brief latency, explosive echo responses accompanied by euphoria or labile emotionality and a lack of awareness for the echoed content; (*2*) echo-like responses with surprise or uncertainty (partial awareness) of the performance; (*3*) repetition with paraphasia, especially phonemic paraphasia, with moderate awareness and efforts at self-correction; and (*4*) complete failure of an anomic type with acute self-awareness, frustration, and at times catastrophic reactions. These several forms of repetition may coexist and alternate in a single patient, just as the Broca's aphasic may have concurrent stereotypy and volitional speech.

The inner relationship between language and awareness is also apparent in the transition from semantic jargon to anomia. A clear progression occurs from the lack of awareness for speech in semantic (asemantic) jargon, through the minimal insight of semantic paraphasia, to the partial awareness of verbal (categorical) paraphasia, and finally to anomia or amnesic aphasia with improved awareness of the speech difficulty. The evolution from a stage of impaired word meaning, lack of awareness, and euphoria to one of perserved word meaning, acute awareness, and frustration occurs gradually through a series of intermediate stages. These stages can be observed from one moment to the next even in the same patient.

From cases such as these of echolalia, stereotypy, or paraphasia, we learn that awareness is linked to the momentary realization level of the utterance and that the *pathological alterations of awareness do not just represent disorders of the normal process, but rather levels that have been achieved.* This assertion, which appears evident in a study of language-bound alterations of consciousness, can also be explored through an investigation of changes in consciousness that accompany more generalized regressive states including the acute confusional state and the derealization complex.

The Confusional State

This condition is easy to recognize but quite difficult to define. There is a disorder of attention with rapid shifts of interest and inability to establish and maintain an attentional set. There is a loosened contact with the surroundings, and the patient seems confused. On direct or multiple choice questions, he is unable to give an account of his location in geographic space (e.g., the hospital, city, or state) or the current date (the day of the week, year, or season). This is referred to as a "disorientation in space and time."

Confabulation may occur and establishes a relationship with the Korsakoff syndrome. While the attentional disorder and the appearance of perplexity in the patient are the most striking features, the syndrome ordinarily—perhaps invariably—occurs along with impairments in memory and affect. The disorder may occur acutely, or it may appear as a stage in the deterioration of a dementia. In either case, however, the disruption is generally uniform across the cognitive level, although the relative emphasis on one or another component may determine special features in an individual case, such as, hallucinations accompanied by a more dream-like or oneiric attitude pointing to a shift toward perceptual systems at the limbic level; excitation, as in manic confusion, pointing to the action component; confabulation pointing to language involvement; and so on.

The awareness of such a patient is intermediate between that of dream and consciousness of self. The patient gives the impression of a closer contact than the dreamer with the shared world around him. Ey (1950) has written that "the essential symptom consists in an incapacity to achieve a sufficient synthesis and differentiation of the psychic contents, which are mixed and agglutinated. This accounts for the lack of lucidity and clarity in the field of consciousness." Since both object and object consciousness develop together, the incomplete resolution and exteriorization of the object will entail an attenuation (failure of development) of consciousness of that object. This is the basis of the impairment of attention. One might say that object consciousness is distributed over the diffuse object field.

The confusional state represents a more or less global dissolution of cognition at the cortical-representational level. The confusion itself is a reflection of the gap between the cognitive level of the patient and that of the examiner and does not truly reflect an inner confusion; in other words, the consciousness experience of the patient is appropriate to his (not the examiner's) genetic level of object formation.

De-realization and De-personalization

The loss of a sense of reality of the object world (de-realization) accompanies the regression of that world back to a pre-object level. De-realization, therefore, may be a partial element of a confusional state, although it may also occur independently, and it points to a deeper level. It is also a sign of incipient hallucination. The incomplete formation and exteriorization of objects leading to a feeling of estrangement from the world is really a partial withdrawal back into the intrapersonal space of imagery.

In de-realization, it is not the object, but rather the object experience, that seems unreal. Federn (1952) has argued that in psychotics the loss of reality of objects is accompanied by a gaining of reality by thoughts. As the object recedes back into the intrapersonal sphere, it becomes more like a thought, while the thought seems to have objectified. This coming to the fore of the cognitive aspect of perception is just another feature of the incomplete object exteriorization. Moreover, this feature helps to bring de-realization into relation with déjà vu. This phenomenon is a kind of brief de-realization, and it points to a predominance in the object of its mnemic (i.e., cognitive) aspect. In other words, déjà vu is the momentary experience of an incomplete object formation. The feeling of familiarity develops out of the greater immediacy with the cognitive matrix within which the object (any object) develops.

In de-personalization, there is a feeling of loss of will, of an inability to go out and meet the (generally de-realized) object world. There is a failure of the action to fully become exteriorized, and, therefore, its imaginal character is regained. This regression is associated with a reduction in the volitional attitude that accompanies the action development. The loss of volition, moreover, entails a greater prominence of more automatic performances.

The anxiety and fear that are a part of de-realization and de-personalization experiences are not simply reactions to the loss of the object or the active self, but they are manifestations at the same cognitive level. Psychoanalytic accounts of estrangement stress the withdrawal of libido from objects. In ego psychology, there is a withdrawal of the libidinal component from the cathexis of the ego boundary. The affective change, however, is not a causal effect or a determining factor, but just another phenomenon that is parallel to the failure of complete object and action development.

De-realization and de-personalization occur in a variety of organic, toxic, and functional states, tending to implicate pathology of the temporal lobes. This is also true of déjà vu experiences. A continuum exists from déjà vu to de-realization and from there to loss of the object world, hallucination, and psychotic regression. Similarly, de-personalization may be a first step toward schizophrenic inertia and loss of will.

These various phenomena are merely partial manifestations of the limbic-presentational level in cognition. The more complete expression of the level occurs in dream or profound psychotic regression. In a sense, therefore, the consciousness of dream and its partial manifestations (as discussed earlier) represent a stage that is preliminary to that corresponding to the confusional state, while the latter is transitional to consciousness of self.

CONSCIOUSNESS AND VOLITION

The various alterations of consciousness that we have discussed can be related to a general model of cognitive formation. According to this model, consciousness is a manifestation of both the achieved cognitive level and the full series of cognitive levels at a given moment in psychological time. Consciousness corresponds to stages in the development of the object world. The realization of an object world has the implication of a *purposeful* behavior in that world. The realization of an object accompanies the actual or implicit realization of an action on that object. This provides the basis for a motility that is *directed toward an object.* In perception, the object appears as an endstage; in action it appears as a goal. In perception, the object is a kind of product that seems to be passive to the act, while in action motility is the product, and it seems to be active in relation to the object. When one perceives in another this orientation of both action and object toward a common goal, the behavior is judged purposeful.

Through language, purposeful behavior can become *volitional*. The distinction here is between an action that is ostensibly directed or motivated toward a goal and an action that is obediant to a will. Purposeful behavior is not necessarily willed behavior, as in trance or fugue states or automatisms, but volitional behavior always incorporates purposefulness. It is in the idea of the will that one sees the microgenetic advance over representational-level cognition afforded by language. Volition is an act of reflection that has an action as its object. Will is a way of describing the self in this reflective state. The problem of volition can be considered not only as an advance over purposefulness, but also in relation to the formation of self.

Volition and the Idea of Self

We have discussed the way in which language is related to mental space just as objects are related to public space, stressing that this is not the old space of imagery that existed before the external world had formed, but rather a space beyond that achieved in the formation of the world. In a very real sense, the initial distinction of world from self leads, through language, to a distinction of self from world. The separation of the world leads only to a consciousness of the world and of self qua object in that world. Self-awareness requires a further differentiation within self. Language fulfills this need. Words do not exist in the world psychologically in the same way as acts or objects do. The object *seems* to exist in itself, to impinge on mind from outside; the action seems to have an effect in that object space. Words "interact" in a different space, and we are conscious of the fact that the word has to be thrown out into that space from its position in the mind. Thus, language begins to populate a new intrapsychic domain. The exteriorization of both object and action provides a common space that can be set against this emerging intrapsychic component. This common space, together with action and object (goal) as purposeful behavior (all of this as a unit, a level in cognition), is incorporated within the experience of volition as a kind of already materialized content beyond (out of) which the language act will emerge.

Another aspect of this transition from purposeful to volitional action concerns the attitude of "activity" created by the very process through which the action unfolds. While the space of perception constantly draws away from the subject, finally "detaching" as the object becomes exteriorized, the subject is drawn into the space of action. This is part of our experience of the temporal or successive nature of action. Seriality brings to action a striving for completion. In contrast to the immediacy of perception, action seems to build up a meaning or a signification over time. The feeling of activity in action development is somehow created through a complex of these factors: the apparent pursuit of meaning, the orientation and progression toward an object, and the temporal unfolding of the action plan. The feeling of activity is then transformed into the idea of an active self. The seriality of action and the increasing separation from the action help to create the deception of a will as causal instigator, and the apparent inexhaustibility of the meaning content of action development gives the impression of actions planned for a future.

The self in a volitional act has to be built up in the same way as any other cognitive component. We have spoken of the cognitive *form* as the experience of consciousness and of the level-specific *components* as determining the conscious content. Self is this content realization together with the awareness form; it is the composite of these two aspects of consciousness. Will is a prominence of self in the context of an action (or an inaction). The corresponding state in perception is reflection or a higher type of object consciousness. Thus, the self in will and the self in consciousness of self (reflection) are expressions of this coming together of the experience and content of consciousness when the latter, the content, is directed toward action or perception, respectively. This orientation, however, concerns the linguistic representatives of action and perception rather than action and perception as such. The consciousness of self in will and reflection is a transformation of the consciousness of activity and objects of a previous level. Consciousness of objects is a consciousness of a world that has already been exteriorized. Self looks on this world of its creation, but this is an earlier self than self in consciousness. In the latter, in reflection, there is a new self and a new object. Self in consciousness of self is related to an idea or image, just as self in consciousness of objects is related to an exteriorized object. All levels in cognition, however, have a share in the self. The traces of innumerable past cognitive traversals, the "selves" of earlier ontogenetic times no longer realized as final contents, the whole body of experience built into structural form, this complex historical and microgenetic organization lies behind, generates, and contributes to the ephemeral self in consciousness.

The Psychoanalytic Theory of Consciousness

A state-specific theory of consciousness is not just a theory of different conscious states, but rather it is a theory of states specific to content and ordered in a series that corresponds to—indeed recapitulates—the formative process through which consciousness develops. Moreover, specificity to content does not refer to the particular content of an act of cognition but to the prominence of certain components (action, perception, language) within that cognitive act. From a variety of conditions, it appears that more than one such conscious state can exist in one individiaul. This is true not only for the more dramatic instance of the "split-brain" patient, but also for dream consciousness, hysteria, dissociative states, and so on, in which contents persist not as "subconscious ideas," but as incompletely realized levels. From the point of view of psychopathology, these levels consist of: (*1*) sensori—motor consciousness, as in sleep, wakefulness, and drive-related states; (*2*) presentational consciousness, where consciousness is in behavior at a preobject level, as in psychosis or dream; (*3*) representational consciousness, where there is consciousness of object and activity, which is disrupted as in the confusional state; and (*4*) symbolic consciousness, where the self, which is realized in consciousness of self (reflection) and will (volition), is threatened with loss, as in depression and apathy, or loss of will.

This concept of pathological levels in a process of realization is, to some extent, incorporated in psychoanalytic formulations of subconscious, preconscious and conscious strata. The emphasis, however, is usually on a two-level system with complex mechanisms of interaction postulated between levels. In contrast, Rapaport (1950 has written, "We have no reason to assume theoretically that these (Cs, subCs) are the only two kinds of consciousness possible. Observation and experience, on the other hand, suggest that there is a group of such states of consciousness ranging between the hallucinatory consciousness characteristic of the dream and waking consciousness (et seq.)." Psychopathological case studies indicate that there is at least one interpolated level. It is likely, however, that any schema of levels will be somewhat arbitrary, the different consciousness states representing phases in the unfolding of cognition rather than distinct systems of consciousness.

According to Freud (SE, 1957, **18**: 7), consciousness and memory do not appear in the same system; instead consciousness arises in place of the memory trace. This notion comes from the view of memory as a deep level store acted upon by other processes. Thus, it is inconsistent with the idea of a "trace" at each level of mnemic realization, that is, that memory is also something to be achieved.

The term ego (*Ich*) generally connotes a province of mind, although it has also been applied to the self or self-concept. In the former sense, the ego (consciousness) is the differentiated surface of the psyche lying between the instincts and perception. Freud (SE, 1957, **19**: 25) says, "For the ego, perception plays the part which in the id falls to instinct. The ego represents what may be called reason and common sense, in contrast to the id, which contains the passions." Thus, ego (self) and consciousness both have a receptive and an inhibitory effect placed between psyche (subconscious) and external world. More recently, Hartmann and others have proposed the idea that the ego has an adaptive role built up around the objects and acts of the real world. Hartmann has rightly called attention to the importance of nonconflictual activity in the ego but, at the same time, has added to the weight of assumed ego functions.

The ego is not a function or a functional division; it is only a possibility, an achievement that must be continually renewed. There are no "ego functions." These are the diverse manifestations of a cognitive level simultaneously realized. The view of ego as a frontier of the psyche thrust against the external world is an application to ego of the conflictual organization of the "lower centers." Conflict points to incomplete resolution and, thus, to preliminary cognition, rather than to interaction and competing interests. The ego does not act in the world. World and ego are represented cotemporally in the same cognitive plane. Ego is not a site where action is initiated; it is the terminal point, the outcome, of an action development.

Ego as self in awareness becomes manifest only when cognition is completely unfolded. At any given moment, however, the endstage cognitive level determines the ego experience, each such level modeling the world up to a certain point. Reality is determined by the degree of modeling achieved. There is no "reality principle," only stages in private space that correspond to levels in the formation of a world that is always "real" to the viewer at each level of its formation. Reality also refers to a shared world that is constructed by all of the members of a group. A concensus concerning this shared world is achieved through access to others inhabiting the same cognitive endpoint.

Some General Considerations

ON FREE WILL

Volition is a stage in the course of an action development, rather than a motive force which stands behind the act. The traditional idea of free will requires an actor or agent who acts. However, since the actor (the self) has, like the action, a developmental history, there is no agent who initiates the action. Both actor and action are realizations of this developmental history.

The idea of free will would also seem to demand that a choice is available to a conscious self. However, the conscious self, or self-in-aware-ness does not cause another cognitive state, it does not choose something but rather gives way to another state rising from below. In a very real sense, each conscious moment dies at the instant of its birth, dissolving away in the continual emergence of new form.

ON THE "MENTAL" AND THE "PHYSICAL"

Mind is not attached to structure but is a kind of organism that undergoes growth and change. Structure is dynamic: Structure is only one brief moment in the life of process. Mind as organic form approaches structure viewed as process. Both mind (or cognition) and structure (or process) unfold according to the same evolutionary law.

Cognition develops over a series of phylogenetic levels. Ontogeny extends the development of both structural and cognitive form. These genetic stages are again recapitulated each moment in cognitive micro-genesis. The process that supports this cognitive form, this series of transformations from one level to the next, is inwardly inseparable from the cognitive form which it supports. This is not an argument for "identity"; it is an argument for parallelism.

The old distinctions between inner and outer and extension and lack of extension do not lead us very close to a solution, or even a true definition, of this problem. Certainly, neuropsychological study seems to confirm a Kantian point of view. Even at the level of retina, the object has undergone some construction, but the final object in perception is no closer to the "real" object than is this retinal construct. At each level in the construction of the world, the "real" object is accurately rendered by cognition. There is no solid physical object waiting to be perceived. Stages in object realization correspond to a hierarchy of physical existences of the "real" object. This "real" world is the stage in cognition that happens to crystallize. In mind, there is no physical *and* psychic; there is only psychic. The physical is an inference about the origins of cognition; it is, therefore, a kind of evolutionary myth.

The model of cognition seems to lead to the following conclusions about the mind—brain problem. The brain process(es) that mediates cognitive development is an *emergent* process that may or may not conform to causal laws. Each brain state is also a mind state, *provided that* the brain state occurs within the framework of the described cognitive structure. There is no additive or one-to-one relationship between brain activity and mind "stuff"; mind is not constructed out of component elements. An isolated, electrically active slab of cortex does not generate a partial mind state. The mind state occurs as an *epiphenomenon* of the brain state when the brain state is both global and embedded in cognitive formation. There is a succession of mind states elaborated as another aspect of (i.e., having the same referent as) a corresponding succession of brain states, but, as epiphenomena, mind states have no influence on these brain states or on other mind states.

ON OTHER FORMS OF CONSCIOUSNESS

Each conscious state in the cognitive series is related to the preceding state as a kind of endstage and to the subsequent state as a ground in which it will develop. A conscious state may, therefore, contain some apprehension of a preceding level, since this preceding level has gone into its (the next level's) formation. There can, however, be no knowledge of a state that lies beyond, since, to any given conscious state, the subsequent state does not yet exist. Thus, waking consciousness has an intuition of the dream experience, but dream consciousness, a more preliminary level, cannot foresee the waking state. From this, it follows that waking consciousness (self in consciousness) could be a point en passage to a still higher stage of which it (waking consciousness) is unaware. It is not inconceivable that certain psychic phenomena, extrasensory experiences and the like, may represent fleeting realizations of this higher level, nor is it inconceivable that such a level of consciousness could participate in some sort of collective fabric. In this respect, the concept of a nöosphere should not be lightly dismissed. Finally, if it is true that every mind state requires a brain state, in addition to the preliminary brain states out of which the final brain state develops, consciousness could not persist independently of brain states. For this reason, it seems unlikely that brain death allows a transcendence to this possible higher level.

9

Creativity

We have seen that the pathological is not a distortion of the normal, but rather a stage through which the normal is achieved. In the same way performance beyond the normal, as in creativity or genius, is not a unique occurrence but, as Goethe said, "only a slight deviation from the ordinary." A study of this "deviation" is of importance for an understanding of normal cognitive structure.

Genius is expressed in both creative and mnemic thinking. These two aspects of cognition, the productive and the reproductive, which have been discussed in relation to thought and memory, although they are part of a genetic continuum, can become quite separated in instances of genius, for example, in artistic or other forms of creative thought as compared to the reproductive prodigy or "idiot savant." If the creative is viewed as a departure from the conventional goal of reproduction, then, in a sense, reproductive thought is the higher performance. This is one reason why the reproductive may be more sensitive to pathology. On the other hand, the creative, at least in the sense of the unusual or unexpected, is a common occurrence in pathological states.

It is important to distinguish the reproductive from the strictly mechanical and the creative from the simply novel. A strong reproductive capacity constitutes a type of genius that differs fundamentally from automatic performance. Reproductive genius often appears precociously in children, but, even in the most restricted cases, such as in mathematical or chess prodigies, there is no sharp differentiation from creative thinking. It is, in fact, this creative origin of reproductive genius that distinguishes it from automatic performance.

The difference between the creative and the novel can be seen in the jargon style of certain poets, Yeats or Cummings for example, and in the jargon speech of aphasics or schizophrenics. Novelty is also achieved in individuals as a type of limited originality. In pathological cases, novelty may point to an inferior cognitive stage, while, in normals, novelty only borrows from this stage. In the latter, novelty is a point on the path toward reproduction, which is really the goal of the thought. In the truly original, the creative, the reproductive is implicit and is something to be surpassed.

By creative we mean more than just a new point of view. Creativity demands the gradual assimilation of cognition in the direction of this new point of view, such that cognition and point of view become inseparable. The process is not dissimilar from that by which the pathological or psychotic patient comes to live more and more completely at the level of the disturbance. In creativity, there is a progressive incorporation of an early stage by a new form or idea. In pathology, an early cognitive stage also comes to dominate the mental life, but there is an inability to go beyond. The degree of genius is determined by the breadth or scope of the original form and by the depth or fullness that the form takes on as it usurps cognition, that is, the extent to which the form becomes one with cognition. This will establish the authenticity or genuineness of the creative idea. In the widest sense, therefore, the creative entails the engendering of organic forms in the mind of the artist and the development of these forms into the living things that are the products of his art.

In this development, the artwork grows organically; it is not pieced together by an artist simply gathering material from the world around him. A work of art is a part of the process of cognition; it recapitulates the microgenetic structure of cognition. Art is a permanent record of the growth of cognitive form. In order to understand this process, however, we must go the artists themselves.

The Beginning of Creative Work

> *Genius has essentially to do with the fact of poetic intuition taking shape in the inaccessible recesses of the soul at an exceptional degree of depth.*
>
> J. Maritain

> *Our thoughts are the bones of our soul. . . .*
>
> M. Maeterlinck

For the psychologist, art is a form of symbolic expression that issues out of cognition as do words and perceptions. For the artist, however, art seems to arise from a deeper layer where ideas and images[1] are less differentiated, richer and more pregnant with meaning. These "inaccessible recesses" where the thought to be first presses into awareness are the crucible in which the final concept of the artwork will be forged. Each thought *seems* to have its beginning in memory. Thus, Nietzsche has written, "Every philosophy has contained an involuntary confession of its creator, a kind of unconscious memoirs. In a similar vein, Dante has said,[2] "Oh mind, that wrote what I saw." Once the memory image is

---

[1] We mean image in the sense of artistic conception, as in Ezra Pound's definition: "An 'image' is that which presents an intellectual and emotional complex in an instant of time."

[2] "O mente, che scrivesti cio ch'io vidi," translated by Grandgent as, "Oh memory, that writest what I saw."

available, however, it is no longer part of the creative work. The memories that the artist recalls are not the fragments out of which the concept will be built; they are the partial expressions of that concept which, at earlier levels, is still in a process of formation. The memory image represents the striving of the concept for reproduction. Through this process of striving and through its final form in memory, in plastic art, or in utterance, the artistic conception is discovered.

Thought is in a continual process of becoming, of seeking itself. The artist does not sort and select the material that will go into the work of art. Rather, this sorting and selecting is itself a product of the artistic conception. In a sense, the thought points to the material needed for its own realization. In this way, the conception expresses itself to the artist. Similarly, in speech, when one gropes for words to express a thought, it is really the thought itself that is groping toward expression.

The first step toward creativity seems to be a deviation at the semantic level. The developing concept must come to live for a time at this level; it must not be prematurely realized, but must gather into itself more and more of cognition at that stage.

Incubation: The Growth of Organic Form

In the development of creative ideas, one requires more than just an original content; a new organization must appear. De Gourmont has written, "In literature, when the form is not new, neither is the content." This development requires a period of inactivity or "incubation." McKellar (1957) cites many examples and points to the advice of Lloyd Morgan: "Saturate youself through and through with your subject . . . and wait." In his celebrated work, Lowes (1927) described how Henry James took a suggestion for the plot of the *The American* and "dropped it for a time into the deep well of unconscious cerebration."

What is this quiet work of unconscious cerebration? Is there, perhaps, a parallel with the common experience that "sleeping on a problem" is an aid toward its solution? Certainly, thought occurs in dream; in fact, some form of thinking may go on continuously throughout sleep. The relation of dream and day fantasy to artistic production is well-known. Freud has written an essay on this subject. This relationship follows from the fact that dreams and dream-like phenomena refer to preliminary cognition. Creativity can also be traced back to the same roots. In both dream and creative thought, the series of semantic fields constituting this level are not rapidly traversed by the forming contents. Cognition persists at this level, enhancing the possibility of a selection of new contents. Of these new contents, some will develop further and will be lost to the level; others will remain and will contribute to the sustained level-specific elaboration. In this way, existing fields are enlarged, distant fields come into new contact, and perhaps even a new field is formed. This may lead eventually to a reorganization of the whole network of semantic interrelationships.

This process is analogous to that of evolutionary selection. Here also the sudden expression of a changed element is generally incompatible with survival. Rather, the new element (a "thought" or genetic mutation) survives only through a slow readaptation or reorganization of the total structure of the organism. Moreover, just as *evolutionary branching* occurs at a preliminary (embryonic) stage in the life history of the organism, creativity also reflects a kind of *semantic branching* at an early stage in cognition. In both cases, the result is a deviation from an otherwise well-traveled path toward representation.

In speaking of unconscious or subconscious cerebration, one should remember that the subconscious is only a term for a phase in thought development prior to content awareness. Maeterlinck has written that "the unconscious and the subconscious are forgotten memories." We would say they are contents incompletely realized. The subconscious, the dream, is a stage in the development of every thought, whether the thought achieves reproduction or an original product.

The "incubation period" thus refers to the time required for this building up of cognitive form, while the "subconscious" or "unconscious" nature of the process refers simply to the consciousness level of this constructive phase. As the process continues, the form gradually enlarges; it seems to fill up with latent content such that expression can no longer be readily achieved. Eventually, a point is reached at which cognition will either be drawn back into the form (i.e., to psychosis) or the content must pass on to a higher level (i.e., to the cortical-representational level) where it reaches the frontier of awareness. The vague intuition of the content in this transitional phase is like the struggling recall of a dream. Unlike a dream that is drawing back to deeper levels, however, the content is struggling out into waking cognition. When this new level is achieved all at once, there is a sudden, global apprehension of the concept in a flood of affect, the moment of inspiration.

Inspiration

In the creative artist, inspiration is a profound and inexpressible experience. Maritain has spoken of "intuitive pulsion" and Frederick Myers of "subliminal uprush." The artistic conception crowds up to the threshold of awareness and declares its richness and meaning. Although the artist speaks of insight, of a "looking-in," *the concept presents itself for discovery.*

An important feature of inspiration is that the concept appears fully formed and complete. The total work is apprehended as a whole and often with irredeemable clarity. Shelley has told us that Milton conceived of *Paradise Lost* as a whole before he executed it in parts. Mozart described his ability to hear a whole symphony in his mind prior to composition. Shortly before his death, Louis Namier saw in his "mind's eye" the scheme of his projected history of the British Parliament. Other examples are given by Koestler (1964) and McKellar (1957). For Koestler, this experience, the "Eureka Process," occurs when two different lines of thought converge. Reverdy has written: "The image is a pure creation of the mind. It cannot be formed from a comparison but from the coming together of two realities more or less separated." The inspiration may be facilitated in some way by a seemingly unrelated thought or experience. One can also say that the final stage of incubation is accomplished through a sudden resolution of the semantic field of the conception.

The sudden appearance of the entire concept in inspiration, its spatial character, immediacy and compresence, the attenuation of consciousness of, and the passivity to the experience are signs that cognition has passed from the semantic to the representational level. We must also consider the feature of ineffability: the concept is too replete for expression, all constituent elements being given at once. This inexpressibility, however, is also a characteristic of representational-level cognition, and, as such, it is analogous to the more restricted case of the anomic patient who also has an abstract representation—a concept—of the word that he cannot express. Moreover, the anomic who finally produces the word will experience the same joy or elation (although in a more limited manner) as that which accompanies inspiration. The affective intensity of inspiration reflects the simultaneous achievement at a preterminal level of all elements of the conception.

In the course of composition, each of these elements must be individually realized. The concept must be revived again and again so that, through partial expressions, the original conception can be rebuilt in the work of art. In this manner, composition also has a restitutive value. It is a means by which cognition can rid itself of the concept; by exhausting the content of this concept, the work of art thus becomes a mode of cognitive recovery.

Composition

> *When composition begins, inspiration is already on the decline.*
>
> Shelley

Composition necessitates the revival of the artistic conception and its completion to a further endstage. This revival may be achieved through a type of concentration that is, in fact, rather a relaxation and regression, or, as in some famous examples, it may be achieved through the contrivance of a certain frame of mind or special mood. Thus, Goethe remarked that Schiller could not write without the smell of decomposing apples which he kept hidden in his desk. Dr. Johnson required a purring cat, orange peel, and plenty of tea to drink. Descartes worked in bed and Buffon only in full dress. This appears to be a general rule in artistic expression and applies to a great many different art forms. Thus, the celebrated grandmaster Tarrasch once declared, "As Rousseau could not compose without his cat beside him, so I cannot play chess without my Kings' Bishop. In its absence the game to me is lifeless and void. The vitalizing factor is missing, and I can devise no plan of attack."

These seemingly makeshift devices are not simply signs of eccentricity. They also accomplish more than a sense of harmony with one's surroundings. A preliminary level in cognition is allowed to come to the fore. In this way, cognition re-enters the level of the original concept. We see this earlier level in the suspension of verbalization, the change from a focal to a diffuse state of attention, the withdrawal from objects to imaginal contents, and the passivity (reduced volitional attitude) to whatever thoughts may appear. Goethe's comment, Thinking doesn't help thought, points to this passive character.

This passivity to thought also produces a feeling of perplexity. There is often a fear that the thought—the Muse—will not come. Dante has written, "Art is the grandchild of God" and Schopenhauer thought that his principle work, *The World as Will and Idea*, was dictated by the Holy Ghost. We see that the artist does not seek the thought; rather, he waits for the thought to present itself to him, and the mood that he strives to recapture is a part of that thought, that concept, and not a state through which new thoughts are inspired.

Although composition may begin at any time, there may be a particular moment before or beyond which composition should not take place. Many artists will refuse to discuss a work that is in progress. There is a feeling that the conception may be exhausted prematurely, and that there is still need for further growth at deeper, form-building levels.

The attempt in composition to recapture the original conception is, however, destined from the start to be a labor of futility. Cassirer (1953) has written, "The more richly and energetically the human spirit engages in its formative activity, the farther this very activity seems to remove it from the primal source of its own being." However, the effort at full expression is essential. The depth and the meaning of a work of art depend on the fidelity of this reconstruction. The authenticity of the work is determined by the adequacy of the expression in relation to the latent content. This also establishes the integrity of the work: its relation to what is organic in human thought. This is why creativity does not require innovation in technique, which is only a different way of exploring or expressing a concept. Genuine creativity is distinguished by an original conceptual form.

Thus, we see that stages in the creative process correspond to stages in cognition. The incubation or growth of the concept at semantic levels leads ultimately to the (at times sudden) emergence of the concept at the representational level. This sequence is repeated again and again in composition as the concept progresses to the symbolic stage and develops into the final work of art. Some evidence for this view can be found in an examination of the effects of brain lesion on creativity.

Creativity and Psychopathology

There are few studies on the effects of brain lesion on creativity (see *Disorders of Language*, Ciba Symposium, 1964). Observations of patients with left hemispheric lesion and aphasia indicate a profound disruption of musical or literary composition. It is unlikely that a composer or writer who has recovered from an aphasia would fully regain his creative power, although compositional skill might remain unaffected. In contrast, there are several instances in which creativity in painting appears to have been heightened after an aphasia. Study of such cases is important for a psychological theory of art.

One striking example of this phenomenon is the noted Bulgarian painter, Zlatio Boiyadjiev, described by Zaimov *et al.* (1964) to whom I am indebted both for the illustrations and for a tour of the canvases at Sofia. One observes immediately in these paintings a striking change from a (pre-aphasic) natural, pictorial, even primitive style with large solid figures and deep earthy tones, to a (postaphasic) richer, more colorful, at times dazzling portrayal with fluid energetic lines and great vigor and inventiveness (see Figure 7). The postaphasic series also shows fantastic, even bizarre, imagery and condensation similar to dream cognition.

Changes of this type may characterize deep-level aphasias. In a case of semantic aphasia (Brown, 1972), drawing became mannered with excessive attention to detail. There was elaboration on and substitution of objects and generally the subjective element held a more prominent position in comparison to previous work. On one test, the patient was given a story to

(a)

(b)

FIGURE 7. Painting by the Bulgarian artist Z.B. before (*a*) and after (*b*) a severe aphasia (Zaimov *et al.*, 1969).

read and illustrate over several weeks. He was instructed to be as economical as possible in his drawing. The story was as follows:

A cowboy went to San Francisco with his dog which he left at a friends while he went to buy a suit of clothes. Dressed in his brand new suit of clothes, he came back to the dog, called it by name and patted it. But the dog would have nothing to do with him in his brand new coat and hat and gave a mournful howl. Coaxing was of no avail so the cowboy went away and put on his old suit and the dog immediately showed its wild joy on seeing its master as it thought he ought to be [Talland, 1965].

Three drawings representing the main sections of the story were produced (see Figure 8). The patient considered these to be accurate renderings of the story line. He could not understand the inappropriateness and tangentiality of certain items, such as the "ranch style" house, the wife for friend, and the car for horse, nor could he eliminate on request inessential details. In the second drawing, the tree takes on a highly subjective flavor reminiscent of that in Zaimov's case, while, in the third, there is a return to the elaboration of the initial illustration. This tendency toward a decorative or purely ornamental elaboration that may submerge the central theme has also been noted in cases of general paresis (Pisarovic, 1968). These alterations appear to be the first stage in a regression to dream-like forms and, thus, are transitional to schizophrenic art.

In contrast to this case, an amateur painter with a phonemic aphasia showed little change except for a tendency toward brighter and more vivid use of color (see Figure 9). This aphasia, however, points to an endstage in cognition, and, therefore, an adequate representation has been already achieved in the artwork.

Through the courtesy of Professor A. R. Luria in Moscow, I recently had the opportunity to examine another painter with phonemic aphasia. This 73-year-old woman was a professional artist, strongly right-handed without a family history of left handedness. She suffered a stroke with right hemispheric lesion and left hemiparesis (i.e., a crossed aphasia) and presented characteristic features of phonemic (conduction) aphasia. Preliminary studies of her sketching, both spontaneously and as illustrations to short stories, demonstrated no apparent alteration in artistic ability.

FIGURE 8. Illustrations of the "cowboy story" by a patient with semantic aphasia, see text.

The loosened semantic boundaries evident in the paintings of certain aphasics recall changes described in psychotic art. Arieti (1975) has noted semantic fusions, stereotypies and mannerisms, and a dream or image-like quality. In progressive psychosis, there is a coming to the fore of increasingly more subjective content. There may also be a repetition of certain themes, reiteration of detail, and loosening of line and contour. Spatial and somatic relationships may also be changed.

In paintings of this type, the frequent condensations and fusions are a sign of semantic-level cognition. The altered sense of space and object place the artwork at a stage prior to the realization of a stable object world. Such observations suggest that pathological art, no less than creative painting, whether fantastic, representational, impressionistic, and so on, refers, in a general manner, to stages in perceptual development.

To my knowledge, there are no comparable studies of the effects of aphasia on sculptors. Bay (1952) has demonstrated that aphasics of various types have difficulty on modeling, chiefly in terms of a reduced and more simplified version of the object. This has been confirmed in a personal study in which aphasics of differing types were required to model three objects in clay; a cup and a bird in response to verbal command, and a cup modeled after the real object. A tendency toward simplification was noted in both motor and global aphasics (see Figure 10). In some cases of jargon aphasia, there was a tendency toward more unusual forms. A patient with a phonemic aphasia produced quite representative objects. The presence of a hemiparesis was not a constant handicap in this group; some hemiparetic patients modeled well with the left hand, while others did poorly.

Evolution of Creative Thought

> *Artistic conception . . . is not a transitional phase of mental evolution, but a final symbolic form making revelations of truths about actual life.*
>
> Susanne Langer

FIGURE 9. Painting by a patient before and after a phonemic aphasia.

This is an important statement that deserves close scrutiny. The issue resolves in part around whether or not a primitive level in thought may serve for the elaboration of highly evolved symbols. In fact, this "primitive" level is common to the art (to the cognition) of children, artists, and psychotics and accounts for the well-known similarities between these groups (Werner, 1940). The child and the psychotic live at this level: in the former, in the course of development, in the latter, as an endstage of regression. The artist, however, moves freely over the range of cognition. Ernst Kris (1952) has described this capacity for productive regression; Koestler (1964) has remarked: "The capacity to regress, more or less at will, to the games of the underground, without losing contact with the surface, seems to be the essence of the poetic, and of any other form of creativity."

From the phylogenetic point of view, the artistic conception can be regarded as a final symbolic form since there is nothing that corresponds to it in the evolutionary history of the species. Moreover, there is a prefiguration of stages that have not yet been reached at that evolutionary level. In the momentary history of the thought, however, the artistic conception is a transitional phase to a still higher level.

A recurrent theme concerns the need for a periodic return to the "pool" of the subconscious for replenishment. Goethe has written, "Man cannot abide long in the conscious realm; time and again he must take refuge in the subconscious, for that is where his roots are." This return is a search for a new beginning; it is not a true return, but rather a desire for new growth. It is a sign that existing concepts are inadequate, that expression has exhausted the meaning content of the conception. The more one lives in the sphere of words, the more need there is to reclaim the conception. Some people are apprehensive of returning to a more primitive level in thinking; there is a fear of fragmentation of the personality. It is, therefore, paradoxical that this very fragmentation is what is overcome by movement into the depths. Hölderlin has written of the attractions and dangers of the creative life. This process of return is so much a part of the needed balance between deep and surface levels that it has been incorporated, as catharsis and renewal, into social custom and mythology (Eliade, 1959).

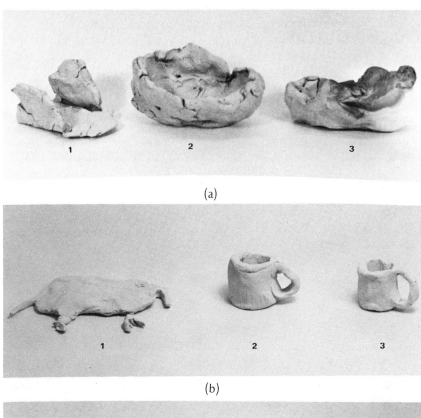

FIGURE 10. Modeling in (a) "motor," (b) "sensory," and (c) semantic aphasia: (1) bird (2) cup with model (3) cup without model.

Art and Meaning

Feeling and meaning come together in signification, but there is a difference. We have feelings, but we strive toward meaning. Feeling is the affective element in signification. Feelings are signposts of the different stages through which the thought passes on the way to expression. Susanne Langer (1967) has written, "Every artistic form reflects the dynamism that is constantly building up the life of feeling." It is also true that every feeling reflects the building up of the artistic form. Meaning relates to a process of expressive realization. It seems also to involve a relationship between what needs to be expressed and what can be expressed and of the adequacy of the expression to the conception. One can say that meaning has to be achieved, that it points toward something. Meaning also seems to become feeling when its aim turns inward, that is, when this outward direction is attenuated. When this occurs, both feeling and meaning are experienced as a "waiting content" in need of expression.

The artist's experience of meaning and feeling differs from that of the viewer. The work of art is given as a whole to the artist, while, in the viewer, the whole has to be reconstructed from parts. There is a different relation to meaning, to signification. Ultimately, however, the signification of the work of art must be experienced by the viewer in order to determine the authenticity of the work. This is not a passive appreciation. The viewer gains meaning to the extent that the artwork is actively created as it is perceived.

In the feeling evoked by a work of art, there is a quality of *meaningfulness*. Perhaps this is why Kris (1952) remarked that great art has a high degree of ambiguity. The ambiguity shows that the work has meaningfulness but does not have a meaning. Feeling seems to receive this meaningfulness as a sudden outpouring. In this way, we see that feeling can be experienced as a kind of compressed meaning.

MacLeish has written:

A poem should not mean But be.

The meaning attached to a poem is provided by the reader through a partial understanding. The reader also perceives meaning as an aim when an incomplete poem achieves a full understanding. Therefore, meaning may develop because an artwork is unfinished or because a finished work is not fully understood. The artwork seems to aim beyond itself: It is not rounded out; it is not filled up or completed by the expression. When the conception of the work is fully embodied in the expression, the expression, such as the poem, can point only to the conception, which is itself, as if a pitcher giving rise out of its own substance to the water within it should become one with the water it creates.

In this way, creative thinking has a relation to the process of becoming that is life itself. Into a world of objects, the work of art comes as a gift. Every great work of art is a presentation to life. The artist does not simply produce new thoughts or new works; he produces organic forms that live and breathe. Schopenhauer has written, "I look at my work, and I say, like a mother: I am blessed with the fruit of my own being." Freud has commented, "Whoever works as an artist certainly feels as a father to his works."

The work of art undergoes a process of incubation and birth as do other living things. Then it takes on a quality of independence from its creator. The new form grows out of the subjective into a world of real objects. For the artist, this is also a process of self-discovery, as thought and thinker strive as one to be more clear, to be more knowable. When the conception behind the work draws completely on the cognitive life of the artist, and when such a conception is fully realized in the work, we can truly say that the artist *is* his thought, his art.

References

Adey, W. EEG Studies of hippocampal system in the learning process. In *Physiologie de l'hippocampé*, Éditions du centre national de la recherche scientifique, Paris, 1962.

Alajouanine, T., Sabouraud, O., & De Ribaucourt, B. Le jargon des aphasiques. *Journal de Psychologie*, 1952, **45**: 158–180, 293–329.

Angelergues, R., Hecaen, H., Djindjian, R., & Jarrie–Hazan, N. Un cas d'aphasie croissée. *Revue neurologique*, 1962, **107**: 543–545.

Arieti, S. *The intrapsychic self*. New York: Basic Books, 1967.

Arieti, S. *Interpretation of schizophrenia* (2nd ed.), New York: Basic Books, 1975.

Arkin, A. & Brown, J. Resemblances between NREM associated sleep speech, drowsy speech, and aphasic and schizophrenic speech. In *Association for the psychophysiological study of sleep*, 1st International Congress Bruges, Belgium, June 19–23, 1971, p. 253.

Babinski, J. Contribution á l'étude des troubles mentaux dans l'hemiplegie organique cérébrale (anosognosie). *Revue Neurologique*, 1914, **27**: 845–848.

Barbizet, J. Études sur la Mémoire. Series 1 et 2, *L'Expansion*. Paris, 1964 and 1966.

Basser, L. Hemiplegia of early onset and the faculty of speech, etc. *Brain*, 1962, **85**: 427–447.

Bender, M., & Krieger, H. Visual function in perimetrically blind fields. *Archives of Neurology & Psychiatry*, 1951, **65**: 72–79.

Betlheim, S., & Hartmann, H. On parapraxes in the Korsakoff psychosis. In D. Rapaport (Ed.), *Organization and pathology of thought*. New York: Columbia Univ. Press, 1951.

Bleuler, E. *Dementia praecox*. (English translation by J. Zinkin) New York: International Universities Press, 1950.

Bogen, J. Presentation at Academy of Aphasia, Rochester, 1972.

177

Boller, F. Destruction of Wernicke's area without language disturbance. *Neuropsychologia*, 1973, 11: 243–246.

Brentano, F. *Psychology from an empirical standpoint.* London: Routledge and Kegan Paul, 1973 (English Edition).

Brown, J. Physiology and phylogenesis of emotional expression. *Brain Research,* 1967, 5: 1–14.

Brown, J. *Aphasia, apraxia and agnosia: Clinical and theoretical aspects.* Springfield, Ill.: Charles C. Thomas, 1972.

Brown, J. Language, cognition and the thalamus. *Confinia Neurologica*, 1974, 36: 33–60.

Brown, J. The neural organization of language. *Brain and Language*, 1975, 2: 18–30.

Brown, J. The neural organization of language: aphasia and neuropsychiatry. In M. Rieser and S. Arieti (Eds.), *American handbook of psychiatry.* Vol 4. New York: Basic Books, 1975a.

Brown, J. The problem of repetition. *Cortex*, 1975b, 11: 37–52.

Brown, J. Consciousness and pathology of language. In R. Rieber (Ed.), *The neuropsychology of language: Essays in memory of Eric Lenneberg.* New York: Plenum, 1976.

Brown, J. Review of: Language communication and the brain. *Linguistics*, 1976a (in press).

Brown, J., & Coleman, R. Hereditary spastic paraplegia with ocular and extrapyramidal signs. *Bulletin of the Los Angeles Neurological Societies*, 1966, 31: 21–34.

Brown, J., & Hecaen, H. Aphasia and the cerebral representation of language. *Neurology*, 1976, 26: 183–189.

Brown, J., & Jaffe, J. Hypothesis on cerebral dominance. *Neuropsychologia*, 1975, 13: 107–110.

Brown, J., & Wilson, F. Crossed aphasia in a dextral. *Neurology*, 1973, 23: 907–911.

Buge, A., Escourolle, R., Rancurel, G., & Poisson, M. "Mutisme akinétique" et ramollissement bicingulaire. *Revue Neurologique*, 1975, 131: 121–137.

Busse, P. *Zeitschrift für Psychologie*, 1920, 84: 1.

Cassirer, E. *The philosophy of symbolic forms.* Vol 1. New Haven, Connecticut: Yale Univ. Press, 1953.

Chapman, L., & Chapman, J. *Disordered thought in schizophrenia.* Englewood Cliffs, New Jersey: Prentice–Hall, 1973.

Clarke, P., Wyke, M., & Zangwill, O. Language disorder in a case of Korsakoff's syndrome. *Journal of Neurology, Neurosurgery and Psychiatry*, 1958, 21: 190–194.

Coghill, G. *Anatomy and the problem of behavior.* London and New York: Cambridge Univ. Press, 1929.

Conrad, K. Strukturanalysen hirnpathologische Falle. *Deutsche Zeitschrift für Nervenheilkunde*, 1947, 158: 344–371.

Conrad, K. Über aphasische Sprachstörungen bei hirnverlezten Linkshander. *Nervenarzt*, 1949, 20: 148–154.

Constantinidis, J., Tissot, R., & de Ajuriaguerra, J. Dystonie oculo-facio-cervicale, etc. *Revue Neurologique*, 1970, 122: 249–262.

Corsi, P. *Human memory and the medial temporal region of the brain.* Ph.D. thesis, McGill University, Montreal, 1972.

Curran, F., & Schilder, P. Paraphasic signs in diffuse lesions of the brain. *Journal of Nervous and Mental Disease*, 1935, **82**: 612–636.

Damásio, A., Lima, A., & Damásio, H. Nervous function after right hemispherectomy. *Neurology*, 1975, **25**: 89–93.

Delay, J., & Brion, S. *Les démences tardives*. Paris: Masson, 1962.

de Morsier, G. Les hallucinations. *Revue d'Oto-Neuro-Ophtalm*, 1938, **16**, 244–352.

Denny–Brown, D. *The basal ganglia*. London and New York: Oxford Univ. Press, 1962.

Dimond, S. *The double brain*. Edinburgh: Churchill–Livingstone, 1972.

Domarus, E. von. The specific laws of logic in schizophrenia. In J. Kasanin (Ed.), *Language and thought in schizophrenia*. Univ. of California, 1944.

Douglas, R. The hippocampus and behavior. *Psychological Bulletin*, 1967, **67**: 416–442.

Eliade, M. *Cosmos and history: The myth of the eternal return*. New York: Harper & Row, 1959.

Ettlinger, G., Jackson, C., & Zangwill, O. Dysphasia following right temporal lobectomy in a right-handed man. *Journal of Neurology, Neurosurgery and Psychiatry*, 1955, **18**: 214–217.

Ey, H. *Etudes psychiatriques*. Vols 1–3. Paris: Desclée de Brouwer, 1950–1954.

Federn, P. *Ego psychology and the psychoses*. New York: Basic Books, 1953.

Fisher, C. Subliminal and supraliminal influences on dreams. *American Journal of Psychiatry*, 1960, **116**: 1009–1017.

Fisher, C., & Adams, R. The transient global amnesic syndrome. *Acta Neurologica Scandinavica Supplement*, 1964, **40**: 7–82.

Foix, C. Aphasies. *Nouveau Traité de Médecine*, Vol. 18. Paris: Masson, 1928. Pp. 135–213.

Foulkes, D. Dream reports from different stages of sleep. *Journal of Abnormal Social Psychology*, 1962, **65**: 14–25.

Freud, S. *Standard edition*. London: Hogarth, 1966.

Froeschels, E. A peculiar intermediary state between waking and sleep. *Journal of Clinical Psychopathology*, 1946, 7: 825–833.

Gardner, R., & Gardner, B. Teaching sign language to a chimpanzee. *Science*, 1969, **165**: 664–672.

Gazzaniga, M. *The bisected brain*. New York: Appleton, 1970.

Gelardi, J., & Brown, J. Hereditary cataplexy. *Journal of Neurology, Neurosurgery and Psychiatry*, 1967, **30**: 455–457.

Geschwind, N., & Kaplan, E. A human deconnection syndrome. *Neurology*, 1962, **12**: 675–685.

Goldstein, K. Analogous mechanisms in the formation of symptoms in organic and functional disorders. *Bulletin of Forest Sanitarium* 1942, 1: 28–36.

Goldstein, K. The significance of psychological research in schizophrenia. *Journal of Nervous and Mental Disease*, 1943, **97**: 261–279.

Goldstein, K. *Language and language disturbances*. New York: Grune & Stratton, 1948.

Goldstein, K., & Katz, S. The psychopathology of Pick's disease. *Archives of Neurology and Psychiatry*, 1937, **38**: 473–490.

Goodglass, H. Studies on the grammar of aphasics. In S. Rosenberg and J. Kaplan (Eds.), *Developments in applied psycholinguistic research*. New York: Macmillan, 1968.

Guiraud, P. *Psychiatrie Generale*. Paris: Librairie le François, 1950.

Head, H. *Aphasia and kindred disorders of speech*. London and New York: Cambridge Univ. Press, 1926.

Hecaen, H. *Introduction à la Neuropsychologie*. Paris: Larousse, 1972.

Hecaen, H., & Sauguet, J. Cerebral dominance in left-handed subjects. *Cortex*, 1971, 7: 19–48.

Herrick, C. *The brain of the tiger salamander*. Chicago: Univ. of Chicago Press, 1948.

Horowitz, M., & Adams, J. Hallucinations on brain stimulation. In W. Keup (Ed.), *Origin and mechanisms of hallucinations*. New York: Plenum, 1970.

Hubel, D., & Wiesel, T. Receptive fields and functional architecture in two nonstriate visual areas (18 and 19) of the cat. *Journal of Neurophysiology*, 1965, **28**: 229–289.

Hunsperger, R. Affektreaktionen auf elektrische Reizung im Hirnstam der Katze, *Helvetica Physiologica et Pharmacologica Acta*, 1956, **14**: 70–92.

Isserlin, M. Aphasie. In O. Bumke and O. Foerster (Eds.), *Handbuch der Neurologie* Berlin: Springer, 1936. Pp. 627–806.

Jackson, H. In J. Taylor (Ed.), *Selected writings of John Hughlings Jackson*. Vol 2. London: Hodder & Stoughton, 1932.

Jaensch, E. *Eidetic imagery*. London: Kegan Paul, 1930.

Jones, E., & Podwell, T. An anatomical study of converging sensory pathways within the cerebral cortex of the monkey. *Brain*, 1970, **93**: 793–820.

Kaada, B. Cingulate, posterior orbital, anterior insular and temporal pole cortex. In *Handbook of Physiology*. Section I, Neurophysiology, Vol 2, Chapt. 55, 1960. Pp. 1345–1372.

Kinsbourne, M., & Warrington, E. Jargon aphasia. *Neuropsychologia*, 1963, **1**: 27–37.

Kleist, K. Schizophrenic symptoms and cerebral pathology. *Journal of Mental Science*, 1960, **106**: 246–255.

Kleist, K. *Sensory aphasia and amusia*. Oxford: Pergamon, 1962.

Klüver, H. *Behavior mechanisms in monkeys*. Chicago, Illinois: Univ. of Chicago Press, 1933.

Koestler, A. *The act of creation*. New York: Macmillan, 1964.

Köhler, W. Relational determination in perception. In *Cerebral mechanisms in behavior*. Hixon Symposium. New York: Wiley, 1951. Pp. 200–243.

Kraepelin, E. *Dementia praecox and paraphrenia*. Livingstone: Edinburgh, 1919.

Kraepelin, E. General paresis, *Nervous and Mental Diseases, Monograph*, 1913,**14**.

Kreindler, A., Calavrezo, C., & Mihăilescu, L. Linguistic analysis of one case of jargon aphasia. *Revue Roumaine de Neurologie*, 1971, **8**: 209–228.

Kris, E. *Psychoanalytic explorations in art*. New York: International Universities Press, 1952.

Langer, S. *Mind: An essay on human feeling*. Vol 1. Baltimore, Maryland: Johns Hopkins Press, 1967.

Lashley, K. The mechanism of vision. *Genetic Psychology Monograph*, 1948, **37**: 107–166.

Lenneberg, E. *Neuropsychologia*, 1975, **13**: 125.

Leonhard, K. Cycloid psychoses—endogenous psychoses which are neither schizophrenic nor manic-depressive. *Journal of Mental Science*, 1961, **107**: 633.

Lewin, K. *A dynamic theory of personality*. New York: McGraw–Hill, 1935.

Lorenz, K. *Evolution and the modification of behavior*. Chicago, Illinois: Univ. of Chicago Press, 1965.

Lowes, J. *The road to Xanadu: A study in the ways of the imagination*. London: Constable Press, 1927.

Lukianowicz, N. Visual thinking and similar phenomena. *Journal of Mental Science*, 1960, **106**: 979–1001.

Lecours, A. Linguistic analysis of paraphasias. In E. Lenneberg(Ed.), *Language and brain: Developmental aspects*. Neurosciences Research Progress Bulletin, 1974, **12**: 555–564.

Luria, A. *Higher cortical functions in man*. New York: Basic Books, 1966.

MacLean, P. Cerebral evolution and emotional processes: New findings on the striatal complex. *Annals of the New York Academy of Sciences*, 1972, **193**: 137–149.

Marcuse, H. Apraktische Symptome bei einem Fall von seniler Demenz. *Centralblatt fur Nervenheilkunde und Psychiatrie*, 1904, **27**: 737–751.

Maritain, J. *Creative intuition in art and poetry*. New York: Meridian, 1955.

Marquis, D. Effects of removal of the visual cortex, etc. *Association for Research in Nervous and Mental Disease*, 1934, **13**: 558–592.

Matussek, P. Üntersuchungen über die Wahnwahrnehmung. *Arch. Psychiat. Nervenkr*, 1952, **189**: 279.

McKellar, P. *Imagination and thinking*. New York: Basic Books, 1957.

Mehta, V. *Fly and the fly-bottle*. Baltimore, Maryland: Pelican, 1962.

Meyer–Gross, W. Discussion on the presenile dementias. *Proceedings of Royal Society of Medicine*, 1938, **31**: 1443–1447.

Nauta, W. Hippocampal projections and related neural pathways to the midbrain in the cat. *Brain*, 1958, **81**: 319–340.

Nielsen, J. Anterior cingulate gyrus and corps callosum. *Bulletin of the Los Angeles Neurological Society*, 1951, **16**: 235–238.

Pandya, D., & Kuypers, H. Cortico-cortical connections in the rhesus monkey. *Brain Research*, 1969, **13**: 13–36.

Pandya, D., & Sanides, F. Architectonic parcellation of the temporal operculum in rhesus monkey and its projection pattern. *Zeitschrift fur Anatomie und Entwicklungsgeschichte*, 1973, **139**: 127–161.

Papez, J. A proposed mechanism of emotion. *Archives of Neurology and Psychiatry*, 1937, **38**: 725–743.

Patterson, A. Emotional and cognitive changes in the post-traumatic confusional state. *Lancet*, 1942, **2**: 717–720.

Penfield, W., & Mathieson, G. Memory. *Archives of Neurology*, 1974, **31**: 145–154.

Penfield, W., & Roberts, L. *Speech and brain mechanisms*. Princeton, New Jersey: Princeton Univ. Press, 1959.

Petras, J. Connections of the parietal lobe. *Journal of Psychiatric Research*, 1971, **8**: 189–201.

Pfersdorff, C. Les catégories du langage aphasique et la dissociation schizophrénique. *Annales Médico-Psychologiques*, 1935, **93**: 1–11.

Pick, A. Aphasie. *Handbuch der normalen und pathologischen Physiologie*, Vol. 15, No. 2. Berlin: Springer, 1931. Pp. 1416–1524.

Pick, A. *Die agrammatischen Sprachstörungen*. Berlin: Springer, 1913.

Pilleri, G., & Poeck, K. Sham rage-like behavior in a case of traumatic decerebration. *Confinia Neurologica*, 1965, **25**: 156–166.

Pisarovic, F. In *Psychiatry and art*. New York: Karger, 1968. Pp. 162–165.

Pötzl, O., Allers, R., & Teler, J. Preconscious stimulation in dreams, associations, and images. *Psychological Issues*, 1960, **7**: 41–54.

Premack, D. Language in chimpanzees. *Science*, 1971, **172**: 808–822.

Pribram, K. Neocortical function in behavior. In H. Harlow and C. Woolsey (Eds.), *Biological and biochemical bases of behavior*. Madison, Wisconsin: Univ. of Wisconsin Press, 1958.

Rapaport, D. On the psychoanalytic theory of thinking. *International Journal of Psycho-analysis*, 1950, **31**: 1–10.

Rapaport, D. Consciousness: a psychopathological and psychodynamic view. In H. Abramson (Ed.), *Problems of consciousness*. New York: Josiah Macy Foundation, 1951.

Riss, W. Overview of the design of the central nervous system. *Brain, Behavior, and Evolution*, 1968, **1**: 124–131.

Riss, W., Pederson, R., Jakway, J., & Ware, C. Levels of function and their representation in the vertebrate thalamus. *Brain, Behavior, and Evolution*, 1972, **6**: 26–41.

Rothschild, D., & Kasanin, J. Clinicopathologic study of Alzheimer's disease. *Archives of Neurology and Psychiatry*, 1930, **36**: 293–321.

Rubens, A. Aphasia with infarction in the territory of the anterior cerebral artery. *Cortex*, 1975, **11**: 239–250.

Rumke, H., & Nijdam, S. Aphasia and delusion. *Folia Psychiatrica et Neurochir. Neerl*, 1958, **61**: 99.

Sanides, F. Functional architecture of motor and sensory cortices in primates in the light of a new concept of neocortex evolution. etc.. In C. Noback and W. Montagna (Eds.), *The primate brain*. New York: Appleton, 1970.

Schachtel, E. On memory and childhood amnesia. *Psychiatry*, 1947, **10**: 1–26.

Schilder, P. Studies concerning the psychology and symptomatology of general paresis. In D. Rapaport (Ed.), *Organization and pathology of thought*. New York: Columbia Univ. Press, 1951.

Schilder, P. On the development of thoughts. In D. Rapaport (Ed.), *Organization and pathology of thought*. New York: Columbia Univ. Press, 1951.

Schneider, C. Über die Unterschiede zwischen schizophrener Sprach und Aphasie. *Zeitschrift fur die Gesamte Neurol. u. Psychiat*, 1925, **96**: 251.

Schneider, G. Two visual systems. *Science*, 1969, **163**: 895–902.

Segarra, J. Cerebral vascular disease and behavior. *Archives of Neurology*, 1970, **22**: 408–418.

Shapiro, M., Post, F., Loefving, B., & Ingris, J. "Memory function" in psychiatric patients over 60. *Journal of Mental Science*, 1956, **106**: 223.

Sherrington, C. *Man on his nature*. London and New York: Cambridge Univ. Press, 1951.

Silberer, H. Report on a method of eliciting and observing certain symbolic hallucination phenomena. In D. Rapaport (Ed.), *Organization and pathology of thought*. New York: Columbia Univ. Press, 1951.

Sperry, R. A modified concept of consciousness. *Psychological Review*, 1969, **76**: 532–536.

Sperry, R., & Gazzaniga, M. Language after section of the cerebral commissures. *Brain*, 1967, **90**: 131–148.

Sprague, J. Interaction of cortex and superior colliculus in mediation of visually guided behavior in the cat. *Science*, 1966, **153**: 1544–1547.

Steele, J., Richardson, J., & Olszewski, J. Progressive supranuclear palsy. *Archives of Neurology*, 1964, **10**: 333–359.

Stengel, E., & Steele, G. Unawareness of physical disability (anosognosia). *Journal of Mental Science*, 1946, **92**: 379–388.

Talland, G. *Deranged Memory*. New York: Academic Press, 1965.

Teszner, D., Tzavaras, A., Gruner, J., & Hecaen, H. L'asymmetrie droite-gauche du planum temporale. *Revue Neurologique*, 1972, **126**: 444–449.

Trevarthen, C. In S. Dimond and J. Graham Beaumont (Eds.), *Hemisphere Function the Human Brain*. London: Elek, 1974.

Victor, M., Adams, R., & Collins, G. *The Wernicke–Korsakoff Syndrome*. Philadelphia: Davis, 1971.

von Domarus, E. The specific laws of logic in schizophrenia. In J. Kasanin (Ed.), *Language and thought in schizophrenia*. Berkeley: Univ. of California Press, 1944.

von Monakow, C. *Die Lokalisation im Grosshirn*. Wiesbaden: Bergmann, 1914.

von Monakow, C. Experimentelle und pathologische-anatomische Unterschungen. *Archiv. f. Psychiat.*, 1885, **16**, 151–199.

von Stockert, T. Aphasia sine aphasia. *Brain and Language*, 1974, **1**, 277–282.

Vygotsky, L. *Thought and language*, MIT Press, 1970.

Weckowicz, T., & Sommer, R. Body image and self-concept in schizophrenia. *Journal of Mental Science*, 1960, **106**: 17–39.

Weinstein, E., & Keller, N. Linguistic patterns of misnaming in brain injury. *Neuropsychologia*, 1964, **1**: 79–90.

Weiskrantz, L. Experiments on the R.N.S. (real nervous system) and monkey memory. *Proceedings of the Royal Society*, 1968, **171**: 335–352.

Werner, H. *Comparative psychology of mental development*. New York: Harper & Row, 1940.

Whitty, C., & Lishman, W. Amnesia in cerebral disease. In C. Whitty and O. Zangwill (Eds.), *Amnesia*. London: Butterworths, 1966.

Willanger, R. Wernicke's encephalopathy. *Acta Neurologica Scandinavica*, 1966, **42**: 426–454.

Woods, W. Language study in schizophrenia. *Journal of Nervous and Mental Diseases*, 1938, **87**: 290–316.

Yakovlev, P. Motility, behavior and the brain. *Journal of Nervous and Mental Diseases*, 1948, **107**: 313–335.

Zaimov, K., Kitov, D., & Kolev, N. Aphasie chez un peintre. *Encephale*, 1969, **58**: 377–417.

Zurif, E., Caramazza, A., Myerson, R., & Galvin, J. Semantic feature representations for normal and aphasic language. *Brain and Language*, 1974, **1**: 167–187.

Index

F4